Fire HD6 / HD7 Made Easy:

A VISUAL User Guide for the Fire HD6 and HD7

Edward Jones

Fire HD6 / HD7 Made Easy:
A VISUAL User Guide for the Fire HD6 and HD7
Edward Jones

Other Books by Edward Jones

Top 300 Free Apps for the Kindle Fire is your guide to 300 of the top rated apps that you'll find useful for your Fire. Jones has taken the time to research and compile this extensive list of apps for your Fire, and best of all, each of these apps are FREE. You'll find apps for the home office, for entertainment, for news, weather, and sports, for your health, for managing your finances, for playing games, and more. A local news apps section provides news, weather, and traffic apps for over 50 major US cities, and a travel section gives you an insight to the best apps that will help you find great deals on flights, hotel rooms, cruises, dining, and even the best gas prices around your hometown or when on the road. Each listing begins with a clickable link back to the Amazon catalog. So as you read this book on your Fire tablet, if any particular app sounds like what you've been looking for, just tap the image or heading name. You'll be taken directly to the Amazon page for the app, where you can click the button to install that app. (Active wi-fi connection required.) Let Top 300 Free Apps for the Kindle Fire be your guide to the best free apps for your new tablet!

Kindle Fire HDX Tips, Tricks, and Traps: A Tutorial for the Kindle Fire HDX. If you happen to own BOTH a Kindle Fire HDX, and a Kindle Fire HD6 or HD7, you may already know that they are *not* the same device. In this comprehensive guide, you'll learn tips (ways to effectively use your Fire), tricks (ways to improve the operation of your Fire), and traps (things to avoid to prevent problems while using your Fire). Learn to use features that are new to the HDX line, including Google or Outlook Calendar and Contacts synchronization, Microsoft Exchange corporate e-mail support, and Amazon's 'Mayday' online technical support. This book also details how you can use the built-in cameras (front-facing in the 7-inch model, front-and-rear facing in the 8.9-inch model) to take photos and videos; how you can setup the security options to protect your account information; and how you can provide a safe environment for children using parental controls and Kindle FreeTime. If you own a Kindle Fire HDX, you owe it to yourself to get the book that's been written *exclusively* for the *Kindle Fire HDX*! *YOU CAN PURCHASE either book by going to www.amazon.com, searching for 'kindle fire edward jones' and clicking the link for the desired title.*

For a complete listing of books by this author, see our website at
www.thekindlewizard.com

INTRODUCTION

So, you've got a Fire HD6 or HD7 as a gift, or perhaps you bit the purchase bullet on your own because you wanted this awesome tablet. However you came into possession of your Fire, you probably have unanswered questions about its operation, or would just love to get the most out of your new tablet. Packed with detailed instructions, numerous tips, and an occasional link to an instructional video, this step-by-step user guide will get you up and running quickly with your Fire HD6 or HD7. You will learn-

- How to get around to the user interface, the home screen, and the carousel more efficiently
- How to make your Fire HD6 or HD7 your own, customizing its display and operation for fastest and easiest use
- How to use the new household profiles feature to allow shared use of a Fire HD6/HD7 by multiple users of the same household
- How to find THOUSANDS of FREE as in, 'zero dollars and zero cents') books
- How to use the built-in cameras to take photos and videos
- How to setup your e-mail accounts, including corporate accounts such as Microsoft Exchange
- How to setup the security options to protect your account information
- How you can move your iTunes or other music library to your Fire
- How you can download YouTube videos to your Fire
- Suggested apps that no Kindle Fire owner should be without

You will learn all of the above and more, with *Fire HD6 / HD7 Made Easy* as a part of your library. Read on, and learn 100% of what you need to know to get the most out of your Fire HD6 or HD7!

IMPORTANT NOTE: This book covers the Fire HD6 and HD7, introduced by Amazon in September of 2014. If you are using any other model of Kindle Fire, please see our sister publications "Kindle Fire HD Tips, Tricks, and Traps," or "Kindle Fire HDX Tips, Tricks, and Traps."

Table of Contents

Chapter 1: Kindle Fire Out of the Box

Welcome to *Fire HD6 / HD7 Made Easy*. As with all books in our *Made Easy* series, this book has been designed from the ground up to get you up and running quickly with your new Fire. You'll find this comprehensive users guide to be packed with clear step-by-step directions, plenty of illustrations to help clarify subjects, and an occasional reference to a tutorial video. Here is where you will find all the basic tips you need to quickly learn to use your Fire like a seasoned pro. And the more advanced topics covered in this book will help you take your use of your Fire to a higher level, getting the most out of your new tablet.

About the Fire HD6 and HD7

The Fire HD6 and HD7 are two products in a line of products known as Amazon Kindles. Kindles are handheld devices, designed and sold by Amazon that let you shop for and view or download e-books, magazines, movies, TV shows, music, and other digital content using wireless technology. The

Fire HD6 and HD7 models were released in September 2014, and are (at the time of this writing) unmatched in terms of outstanding features at a very affordable price. The Fire HD7 sports a 7-inch display and built-in stereo speakers with Dolby sound for audio playback, while the Fire HD6 offers a slightly-smaller 6-inch screen and a single mono speaker. Both models represent a significant amount of tablet for the money, with prices starting at under $140 US for the HD7 and under $100 for the HD6 at the time of this writing. The Fire HD6 and HD7 are two models within the Fire family, the others including the Fire HDX, in both 7-inch and 8.9-inch (diagonal measurement) screen sizes.

Amazon's Fire product line has been in existence for some time, with the first models introduced in 2011. Until September 2014, all products within the line were referred to under the name 'Kindle Fire.' With the September 2014 introduction of new models (including the Fire HD6 and HD7), Amazon has dropped 'Kindle' from the names of the products, instead referring to all devices with color screens under the name 'Fire' (Fire HD6, Fire HD7, Fire HDX 7, and Fire HDX 8.9). Amazon now uses the name 'Kindle' exclusively for its e-ink (non-color) line of book readers, including the Kindle Touch, Kindle Paperwhite, and Kindle Voyager. This book refers to your device as the Fire HD6 or Fire HD7, but you are likely to see it referred to as a 'Kindle Fire HD6' or 'Kindle Fire HD7' at web sites and in other publications.

About tablet computers

The Fire HD6 and HD7 fall price-wise at the low end and feature-wise in the midst of handheld computers generally referred to as tablets, and tablets occupy the market space between smartphones and laptop computers. Tablets generally possess all or nearly all the functions of laptop computers, two notable exceptions being that tablets generally lack physical keyboards and have smaller screens. The appealing feature of tablet computers is that they can run "apps." Apps, short for applications, are small computer programs that run within the tablet's internal memory and literally re-define the operation of the tablet. Apps can give your Fire the ability to act as far more than an e-book reader or a movie player. You can download and install apps that transform your Fire into a digital butler, an electronic medical advisor, a powerful financial analyst, or a first-rate handheld game platform.

Where's My Data? (Your Fire, Storage, and the Amazon Cloud)

With the popularity of tablets, you may have heard talk of what may be a somewhat magical and mystical place known as "the cloud." Your Fire has some built-in data storage of 8 gigabytes or 16 gigabytes, depending upon the memory option you chose when you purchased your Fire (8 gigabytes being the standard amount).

This may sound like a lot of space, but in the grand scheme of things, it really is not. (By comparison, the average personal computer sold at the time of this writing typically has a 500 gigabyte or 1,000 gigabyte or "one terabyte" hard drive, and a single Blu-Ray DVD movie occupies roughly 25 gigabytes.) If you tried to store large amounts of digital content- especially movies and videos- on your Fire, you would quickly exhaust its usable space. To get around this problem, all Amazon Fires (and many other tablets) store large amounts of information in the cloud, which is another name for data servers that are accessed from the Internet. Amazon's servers are referred to as the Amazon Cloud, and all Fire owners have access to unlimited amounts of data storage for their purchases in the Amazon cloud. You can also store your personal data in the Amazon Cloud, with up to five gigabytes of free storage assigned to your Amazon account.

Content that you purchase from Amazon is stored in either of two places: in your cloud storage on Amazon's servers, and on your Fire itself. (Often, your content is stored in two places simultaneously: when you download an item, it is stored both on your device, and a copy of it remains in the Amazon cloud.) When you initially purchase a book, a song, a game, or an app (even free content is purchased, you just aren't charged for this), the content is initially stored in your personal space in the Amazon Cloud, where the content is not taking up any space on your Fire. When you press the Download button that appears on the icon for that content in the cloud, it gets downloaded to the memory space of your Fire itself.

Check out the Amazon Help Video.

Amazon has taken the time to provide a short help video explaining how your Fire works with the Amazon Cloud. You can view the video at the Amazon web site. Point a web browser at www.amazon.com/help and at the page that appears, click "Fire, Kindle and Echo" on the left, then click "Fire HD and HDX Tablets" on the right. At the next page, under "Getting Started," click "Fire Tablet Help Videos," then click "Syncing and the Cloud."

If you display a given category on your Fire, such as apps, books, or music, at the top of the screen you will see icons for *Cloud* and *Device*, as shown in the illustration that follows.

Tap CLOUD to see what is stored in the Amazon cloud.   **Tap DEVICE to see what is stored on your Fire.**

(Images used in artwork courtesy Amazon, Inc. unless otherwise noted.)

Tap Cloud to see all of the content that is stored on Amazon's cloud under your account, and tap Device to see all the content that you downloaded from the cloud onto your device.

You can download content from the cloud onto your device anytime you have an active Wi-Fi connection, and you can delete content from the device as necessary to ensure that you have plenty of room for new content.

If you are curious as to whether you are running short of storage space on your device, you can quickly determine your available storage space remaining. To check this amount, do this:

1. Get to the Home screen.

2. Tap and drag down the Navigation bar at the top of the screen.

3. Tap Settings at the upper right.

4. Tap Device Options at the next screen that appears.

5. Tap Storage. You will see a Storage screen (see illustration).

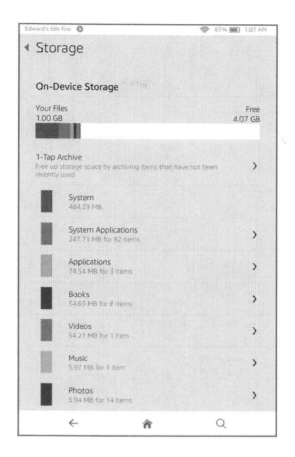

The Storage screen tells you how much space is available, and how much space is currently being used by various categories, such as books and newsstand items, audio books, music, videos, and photos.

Setting up your Fire

> **1. Set up your Fire now if it is fresh out of the box.** If you've just opened up your Fire's box, you'll need to turn it on and set it up. Before you start, make sure you have your Amazon username and password, and you will also need to be within range of an active Wi-Fi connection.

2. When you first turn your Fire on, you'll be asked to choose your language. After doing this, you'll select a Wi-Fi network and enter a password (if yours is a secured network).

3. The next screen that appears will ask you for registration information. You'll now need to register your Fire. Enter your Amazon account details, or, if you don't have an Amazon account, choose create an account and follow the instructions that appear on the screen.

4. Next, you'll get to choose your time zone, and confirm your account information. Make your selections and tap Continue, and you will be asked if you wish to enable automatic backup to the Amazon cloud. This is recommended by Amazon, as the automatic backup feature keeps any files that you create on your Fire, such as pictures and videos you shoot, as well as music that you may add to your device.

5. After choosing whether to enable automatic backup, you will be given the option to set up your Facebook and/or Twitter accounts. (You can do this now, or skip this step and save this for later.)

6. Finally, you will see some on-screen hints and tips that will help you get started with your Fire. If you already have Kindle content linked to your device, or apps from the Amazon App Store, they will all be available for download from the Amazon Cloud (more on this topic shortly). Your recently-read Kindle books will appear in an area known as the carousel automatically, along with the latest apps and other downloaded content.

Controls and Layout of the Fire HD6 and HD7

Take the time to get familiar with the physical aspects of your Fire. Looking at the front of the device, with the volume rocker switch at the upper right, the following illustration shows the layout of various components.

Fire HD6 and HD7, front view (artwork courtesy Amazon, Inc.)

If you own a Fire HD6, the rear of your device looks like this:

Speaker (mono)

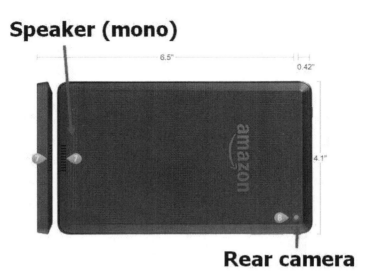

Rear camera

Fire HD6, rear view (artwork courtesy Amazon, Inc.)

And if you own a Fire HD 7, the rear of your device looks like this:

stereo speakers

rear camera

Fire HD7, rear view (artwork courtesy Amazon, Inc.)

Get familiar with the various parts of the Fire's user interface. The next chapter will detail this area extensively, but out of the box, it helps to know about the areas that you will be working with on your Fire's screen. The following illustration shows these areas.

Device Name · Wi-Fi Indicator · Batttery Life · Current Time

Edward's 6th Fire   🔊   📶 83% 🔋 1:06 AM

Games   Apps   Books   Music   Videos   Newsstand   Audiobo

(upper part of Fire's screen)

Navigation bar

Search icon

Carousel

Offers from Amazon

Favorites

(Fire HD6 / HD7 display)

Get quick access to items that you use regularly by placing them in your Favorites area. (You can view all of your favorites by swiping the entire screen upwards with one finger.) To add a book, periodical, or app to your favorites area, do this:

1. Tap he desired category on the the Navigation bar at the top of the screen.

2. When the category appears, press and hold a desired item until a highlighted menu bar appears at the top of the screen.

3. Tap the Home icon in this area.

NOTE: To install any saved apps, in the Navigation Bar tap on Apps, then tap on the Cloud tab. Tap on any of the icons to start that particular app downloading onto your device.

Having problems??? When in doubt, reboot. Your Fire is a sophisticated computer, and like all computers, it may hiccup for unexplainable reasons at times. If your Fire freezes or locks up and refuses to respond to any actions, perform a hard reset. (You needn't worry about losing any memory settings with this type of reset; it just halts any programs currently running and shuts down your device.) Hold the power button depressed until you see a 'Shutdown your Fire?' message appear on the screen, and then tap Yes.' Wait another 10 seconds, then turn on your Fire

If you are experiencing an unusually high number of system lock-ups, make sure your battery charge level is not very low. A nearly fully-drained battery is a common cause of random Fire freezes.

Chapter 2: Navigating on your Kindle Fire

Unlike traditional laptop and desktop computers, tablets use a different means of interacting with the *user interface* (that's techno-speak for "the way you get along with the device"). With tablets, your primary means of using the device is to touch the screen using a variety of finger movements in response to what you see on the screen. You will be able to use your Fire in a more efficient manner if you are familiar with the arrangement of your Fire's user interface

About the Home Screen, Navigation Bar, Carousel, and Favorites

In this chapter, we go into more detail about the parts of the Fire user interface, and how you can best use these features.

(The Home screen of the Fire HD7)

From the Home screen, your books, apps, music, and videos are all accessible with a swipe of the *Navigation bar*.

Swipe the Navigation bar to the left or right and tap the desired category such as apps, games, books, music, or videos to display all of the items within that category. At the far left of the Navigation bar, there is a **Search icon** (in the shape of a magnifying glass) that can be used to search the entire device content, to search Amazon's massive library of content, or to just search the web.

Check out the Amazon Help Video.

Amazon has taken the time to provide a short help video for this topic. You can view the video at the Amazon web site. Point a web browser at www.amazon.com/help and at the page that appears, click "Fire, Kindle and Echo" on the left, then click "Fire HD and HDX Tablets" on the right. At the next page, under "Getting Started," click "Fire Tablet Help Videos," then click "Navigating your Fire."

The Carousel

The center area of the Home screen displays the *Carousel*. The Carousel will contain an assortment of icons for all of the items that you've recently accessed on your Fire, whether they are books, songs, magazines, movies, or web pages.

Carousel
(Displays recently-viewed books, movies, tv, games, and apps)

TIP **Clean up your Carousel.** Over time, your Carousel can become overly cluttered with icons for all the items you've accessed on your Fire. To delete items from the carousel, press and hold the unwanted item until a menu of icons appears at the top of the screen, then tap the Remove icon in this area.

TIP **Understand the difference between the _Carousel_ and your _Favorites_.** The Carousel grows dynamically as you use your Fire, because an icon for everything that you've recently used on your Fire will appear on the Carousel and will remain for some time unless you delete it from the Carousel. With your Favorites, on the other hand, nothing appears automatically. You must add an item to the Favorites area in order for it to appear. (On a new Fire, it's true that a few items appear in the Favorites area, but Amazon added these items so that the Favorites would not be empty. Clearly, these are not your favorites, so you'll probably want to get rid of them.)

Displaying your Favorites

Whenever the Home screen is visible, to display all of your favorites, do this:

1. Swipe upwards on the entire screen to bring your favorites into view.
2. Tap any favorite to open that item.

You can get quick access to items that you use regularly by placing them in your Favorites. You can view all of your favorites by swiping the entire screen upwards with one finger. To add a book, song, movie, game, or app to your favorites area, first use the Navigation bar at the top of the screen. When the desired category appears, press and hold a desired item until a menu of icons appears at the top of the screen, then tap the Home icon in this area.

Know how to come home. One of the first things any young child learns is how to come home, and any new Fire user should know how to get to the home screen as well. From anywhere you are at, tap in the center of the screen, and the home icon will appear at the right side of the screen; the icons are depicted in the following illustration. Tap Home and you will return to the home screen.

Setting your Display

Adjust your font sizes to make reading easiest on YOU. Your Fire is a great multimedia device, but the entire Kindle line began life as an e-book reader, and millions of people still use it primarily for that purpose. You can easily adjust the font sizes to fit your needs.

> With any book open, tap in the center of the screen, and then tap the View (Aa) icon at the top of the screen. You will see a dialog box like the one shown in the following illustration:

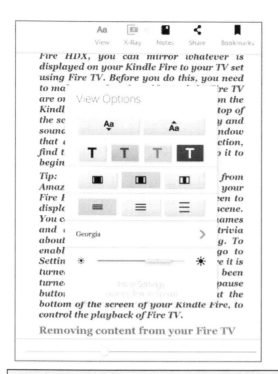

Tap the small letters 'Aa' to shrink the text, or tap the large letters 'Aa' to enlarge the text. You can also try the different Color Mode settings (white, soft green, sepia, and black) to see if you prefer one of these different backgrounds for your book reading. The lower rows within the dialog box contain buttons that let you adjust the margin width or the line spacing. And you can tap the Font name list box (displaying 'Georgia' in this illustration) to display additional fonts that you can choose for your display.

Tap the 'More Settings' link at the bottom of the dialog box, and another screen appears where you can choose to turn on Popular Highlights and Text-to-Speech options. These options, enabled by the publishers of some books and periodicals, allow for the display of highlighted items that other readers find to be popular, and allow for the reading of text aloud, using the built-in speakers or the headphone jack of your Fire.

Note that the Kindle display settings will control the text display of most e-books, but may not have an effect on some magazines. Many of the magazine publishers use their own settings menus to change the way the magazine is displayed.

Customizing your Favorites

Any items that you recently accessed will appear on the Carousel. You can add any of these items to your Favorites so that you can gain fast access to regularly used items by swiping the entire screen upwards. Then do this:

Find the item in your Carousel, press and hold until a large check mark appears in the center of the items image, and then press the 'Home' icon that appears at the top of the screen.

Customize your Favorites to match what YOU want. Just long-press on an item until it dims in brightness, then slide your finger to a new location. The remaining favorites will automatically rearrange themselves.

TIP **Use 'Search' to find anything stored on your Fire**. While many Fire users think of the search field as a way to search for content such as books or movies, you can actually use the Search field to find any item that is stored on your device. Just go to the Home screen, tap the magnifying glass to bring up the Search field, and type a few letters. Search will bring up all items- books, videos, music, games, and so on- that match the letters you've typed. Tap anywhere above the keyboard to put the keyboard away, scroll to the desired item, and tap the item to open the item or launch an app.

Adding household profiles

A major addition to the newest Fire products is the ability to create household profiles, letting you share a single Fire HD among multiple members of your household. (The improvement is actually a part of the new Fire 4.0 operating system, so if you own any 4th-generation Fire such as the HD-6 or HD-7, or any 3rd-generation Fire that has received the Fire 4.0 OS update, you can make use of this feature.) You can add one adult and up to four children as members with their own profiles. With household profiles implemented, the carousel, favorites, and content that each household member sees are unique to that individual.

Check out the Amazon Help Video.

Amazon has taken the time to provide a short help video explaining household profiles. You can view the video at the Amazon web site. Point a web browser at www.amazon.com/help and at the page that appears, click "Fire, Kindle and Echo" on the left, then click "Fire HD and HDX Tablets" on the right. At the next page, under "Getting Started," click "Fire Tablet Help Videos," then click "Household Profiles."

NOTE: If you are adding an adult, that person will need to log in with their own Amazon account credentials to complete the process. Make sure that persons' account information is available before continuing with these steps. (Child profiles will not need their own Amazon accounts.)

Creating an adult profile

To create a household profile for an adult, do this:

1. Swipe down from the top of the screen.
2. Tap Settings.
3. Tap Personal Profiles.
4. Tap Add Adult. You will see the 'Add Adult Profile' screen (see illustration).

The adult must now log in using their Amazon account credentials, or create a new account if they do not have their own Amazon account. Fill in the information needed for the adult profile, and tap Next. You can then proceed to add child profiles if desired, using the following steps.

Creating a child profile

To create a household profile for a child, do this:

1. Swipe down from the top of the screen.
2. Tap Settings.
3. Tap Personal Profiles
4. Tap Add Child. You will see the 'Add Child Profile' screen (see illustration).

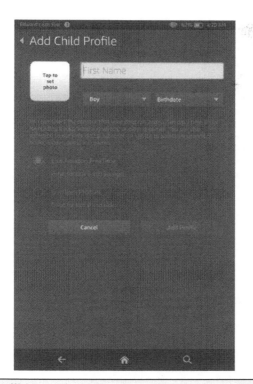

You will be asked to enter the child's name, birthday, and gender. You can also tap the picture icon at the upper left to choose a pre-selected image to identify the child at the login screen, or you can tap 'User photo' to select a personal photo from the gallery. You will also need to select whether the content within the child's profile should be limited by Kindle FreeTime, or whether the profile should be a less-restrictive teen profile. Fill in the requested information, and tap 'Create profile' to add the child profile to your Fire.

Once a child profile has been created, an additional screen will appear (see the following example), and you must approve the content that will be made available to the child.

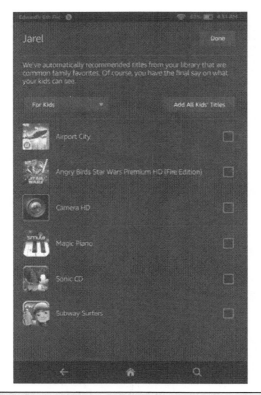

Tap the drop-down menu at the upper-left and choose from 'Books', 'Videos', 'Apps', or 'All' to display your content, then check the boxes beside the content that you want made available to the child. When finished, click the 'Done' button at the upper-right.

Switching profiles

You can switch between profiles by simply turning your Fire tablet off and back on. Press the power button twice, to turn the tablet off and back on. Tap the profile icon that now appears in the upper-left corner of the screen (as shown in the following illustration), then tap the icon for the profile that you wish to use. (If you are switching to an adult profile, you will be prompted for the lock code for that profile.)

Editing or removing household profiles

Once household profiles exist, you can edit or delete a given profile. To do so, swipe down from the top of the screen and tap Settings, then tap Household Profiles to display the household profiles screen, shown here.

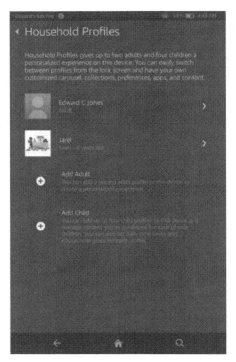

Tap the profile that you want to change, and make the desired changes. (When a profile is visible, you can tap 'Remove from household' to remove the profile, likely the appropriate action to take once your "child" has departed for college!)

WARNING: If you remove an adult profile from a household, that adult's Amazon account cannot be added to another set of household profiles for 180 days.

Household profiles make shared use of a Fire tablet a simple matter. One point that you'll want to keep in mind regarding child profiles is that as your children grow older and as you purchase new content, you'll likely want to update their profiles accordingly.

Changing Basic Settings on your Fire

At the top of your Fire, just above the Navigation bar, is an area known as the Status bar. Here, you will see any notifications indicated by a number inside a small circle, a wi-fi signal strength indicator, and the battery life indicator.

Tap and drag down anywhere within the Status bar area to reveal various settings for your Fire, as shown in the following illustration:

Auto-rotate: your Fire contains a gyroscope, which senses when the device is rotated, causing the display to shift between portrait and landscape mode. There are times when this is more of an annoyance than a help, such as when you are reading with the Fire lying on a flat surface such as a tabletop. Tap the Auto-rotate icon to change the setting to 'rotation-locked,' to disable the auto rotate function.

Brightness: tap the brightness icon to reveal a slider bar that you can slide up or down to increase or decrease screen brightness.

Wireless: Tapping the wireless option brings up another screen with these options:

Tap Wi-Fi to turn on (or off) Wi-Fi, and to choose a Wi-Fi network from a list of nearby networks (see illustration)

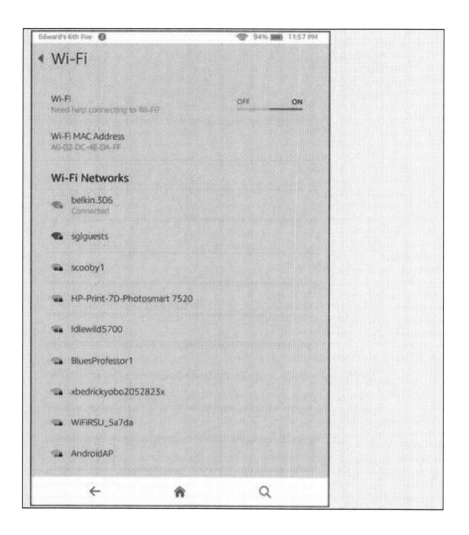

On this screen, select the desired Wi-Fi network by name. If the network is protected, you will be asked for the security key, and you must enter the security key before your Fire will connect to your Wi-Fi network.

Tap Airplane Mode to enable or disable Airplane Mode (turning off wireless transmission for when you are using your Fire in flight)

Tap Bluetooth to enable Bluetooth device settings (for sharing data with other Bluetooth-equipped devices such as many modern laptops, portable keyboards, and some smart phones).

Tap VPN to access settings for Virtual Private Networks which can be used to securely connect to virtual private networks used by many businesses (see your company's network administrator for details)

Tap Location Based Services to allow or prevent Location Based Services from estimating your location.

Check out the Amazon Help Video.

Amazon has taken the time to provide a short help video on the subject of settings for your Fire You can view the video at the Amazon web site. Point a web browser at www.amazon.com/help and at the page that appears, click "Fire, Kindle and Echo" on the left, then click "Fire HD and HDX Tablets" on the right. At the next page, under "Getting Started," click "Fire Tablet Help Videos," then click "Settings."

TIP If you don't remember what the security key is for your own home Wi-Fi network, look on the bottom of the cable modem or the phone company router that provides your Wi-Fi service. Many Wi-Fi routers provided by cable and telephone companies have the password written on a sticker on the underside of the modem.

Quiet Time: This option lets you turn on "quiet time," disabling any popup notifications and muting all sounds for message notifications such as e-mail or calendar alerts.

Help: This icon, when pressed, displays a help screen that lets you get help with wireless connectivity issues, open the user guide for your Fire tablet, or contact Amazon customer service, either via e-mail or by phone.

Settings: Tapping the settings icon will display a settings screen, as shown in the example that follows.

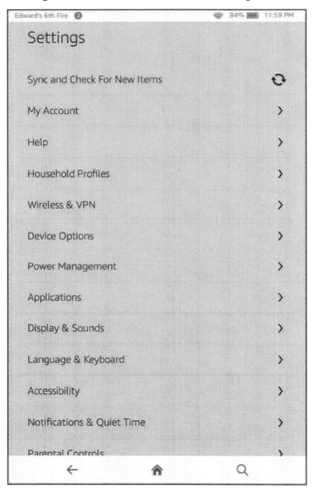

From here, you can access a variety of settings for your Fire tablet, by simply tapping on the appropriate subcategory within the Settings screen. For example, you can tap the Display and Sounds subcategory to display a screen that lets you adjust the volume and or the screen brightness, and you can tap the Security subcategory to create a locking password that prevents your Fire from being used by unauthorized users who do not know the password that you set for your device.

You'll find many of these individual subcategories and their options explained in further detail in later parts of this book.

Of particular interest is the Device Options subcategory under the Settings screen. (To get here, drag down the Notifications bar at the top of the screen, and tap the Settings icon at the upper-right. In the Settings screen, tap Device Options to reveal the screen shown in the following illustration.) Here you can gain access to a number of settings that govern the individual behavior of your Fire HD6 or HD7.

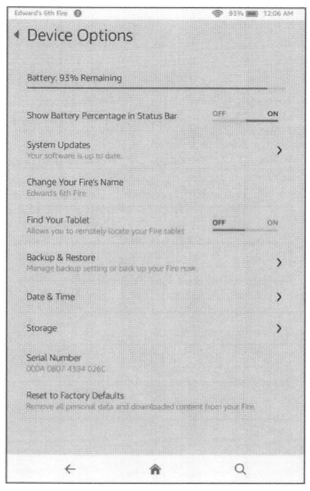

The Device Options screen provides a visual indication of the state of your battery charge, options for changing your tablet's name and finding your tablet remotely, and the storage space utilized by various applications such as books, magazines, movies, music, and so forth. You can perform backup and restore operations from the Amazon cloud, adjust your date and time settings, and even reset the device to its original factory settings (useful when it is time to upgrade to a more powerful Fire HDX, and pass on your trusted Fire HD6/7 to a close friend or relative).

If you return to the settings screen, you will see a number of options for controlling the overall behavior of your Fire. A few of the more popular options on this screen are described below:

Sync and check for new items: -tapping 'Sync and check for new items' icon will synchronize the content of your Fire with the Amazon Cloud, and your email, contacts, and calendar will be synchronized with external sources, assuming you have set up these external sources. Also, note that you can find out how to setup the external sources such as your e-mail, contacts, and calendar in Chapter 7, Fire Email, Contacts, and Calendar.)

Display and Sounds: -tapping 'Display and Sounds' displays another screen with slider bars for volume and display brightness on the screen, and you can finger swipe the slider bar left or right to increase or decrease the volume or the screen brightness (although it's admittedly easier to adjust the volume simply by pressing the buttons on the side of the device.) Use the Display Sleep option to change the time length, in minutes, before the device goes to sleep during periods of inactivity, and use the Font Size option to change the default font size used for text displayed outside of books and magazines (such as in the menus and dialog boxes presented by the operating system).

Language and keyboard: -tapping 'Language and keyboard' causes another screen to appear, containing options that let you set the language used for display of menu items and of the text displayed on all system screens. You will also find options for changing various keyboard settings, and options for pairing a wireless Bluetooth keyboard.

General Typing and Text-Entry Tips

TIP **Make the keyboard larger.** Most Fire apps work in portrait or landscape mode, and the keyboard is much larger and easier to use in landscape mode. Rotate the Fire 90 degrees to get a landscape view of the keyboard, for an easier typing experience.

TIP **When typing large amounts of text, end each sentence with a fast double-space.** Heavy duty word processing on a Fire (or any similarly sized tablet) is going to be somewhat challenging due to the combination of a soft keyboard and small screen size. One time saving tip when doing a lot of typing on the Fire is at the end of each sentence, tap the spacebar quickly twice. A fast double-space will automatically insert a period, followed by a single space. You can then continue on to the next sentence.

TIP **Use the 'predictive keyboard' feature to quickly type entire words.** As you are typing text, you will notice a series of words appears just above the top row of the keyboard. These are words representing your Fire's best guess as to what you are typing, as shown in the following illustration:

-typing 'agree' results in word choices that include 'agreed', 'agreement', 'agreeing,' and 'agreeable.

At any point, you can tap one of the word choices to add that word to your sentence.

TIP **The Fire really does have a Caps Lock key.** For those times when you need to type a string of characters as ALL UPPERCASE LETTERS, the Fire does have the equivalent of a PC's Caps Lock key. Just double-tap the Shift key, and a square block will appear around the Shift symbol on the key indicator indicating that you are in Caps Lock mode. Type your upper case letters, then press the Shift key once more to drop out of Caps Lock mode.

TIP **Use the numbers shortcut to quickly enter numbers**. If you are typing text, you don't need to switch between the letters keyboard and the numbers and symbols keyboard just to enter a number. The top row of letters can be long-pressed to enter a number. From left to right, a long-press on any of the top row of keys produce numbers from 1 through 9, followed by 0. Press and hold a top row letter until a number appears above the depressed key, then release, to type that number.

TIP **Your finger can serve as an insertion pointer**. When editing large amounts of text, tap your finger on any empty area to display the Editing Tool. You can then press on it and move your fingertip within the text that you already typed, then release and edit the text as desired. When done editing, tap again at the end of the text, and continue typing.

TIP **Access the Cut-Copy-and-Paste options with a long-press on any word.** If you need to cut or copy and paste during text editing, long-press on any single word, and cut / copy / paste editing options will appear, along with two selection handles. Drag the selection handles to highlight the desired text, then long-press on the desired text, and choose Cut or Copy. To paste the cut or copied text elsewhere, just long press at the desired location, and tap Paste.

Chapter 3: Shopping for Content for your Fire

Amazon has integrated the Fire to provide a first class shopping experience through the Amazon stores. (The phrase 'stores', plural, is intentional, because with the company's growth, Amazon has divided their online retail store into a collection of stores.) You can think of it as having all of the convenience of a mall-- different stores, each specializing in carrying a broad assortment of products in a specific area-- with none of the disadvantages of a mall (noisy crowds, unruly teenagers, or bad food at the food court). At the time of this writing, Amazon has divided its digital stores into eight categories: books, music, videos, newsstand, apps, games, audiobooks, and Amazon Prime. At the Home screen, tap Shop, and you will see links for the different stores at the left side of the page that appears, as shown in the following illustration.

      To make shopping easier, you will probably want to set up 1-Click ordering as a payment method. 1-Click ordering places your order automatically, letting you skip the hassle of a digital shopping cart. When you place your first order at Amazon and enter a payment method and shipping address, 1-Click ordering is enabled automatically. If you click Buy now with 1-Click on any product page, your order is automatically charged to the default payment method registered to your account, and it is shipped to the default address.

You can also use 1-click to ship to multiple shipping addresses. Perhaps you wish to have some items shipped to you at your job, others at your primary home, and some at your vacation home. Login to your Amazon account through a web browser, and click Manage Your Account. At the next screen, click Manage Addresses and 1-Click Settings. At the next screen that appears, you can enter more than one shipping address.

When you save multiple shipping addresses, and you order an item, a list box with all of your addresses will appear. You can then choose the desired address to have the item shipped to that location.

Note: You must have cookies enabled within your computers' web browser to use 1-Click shopping. ("Cookies" are small chunks of data stored by your browser which are used by Amazon, as well as by many online banks and stores, to identify your account.) If you have not enabled cookies within your browser, you can still purchase items by adding them to the Amazon Shopping Cart, and clicking Proceed to checkout when you are ready to complete your order.

Buying books, magazines, and periodicals

Once you've connected wirelessly and you've set up your 1-click payment option at Amazon, you can easily purchase books, magazines, and newspapers from Amazon, and automatically download your purchases to your Fire. Use these steps to purchase content:

1. At the top of the screen, tap the **Home** ⌂ icon,

2. In the Navigation bar tap **Shop** to display the Amazon Kindle Store.

3. Browse among the various categories or search for items using the Search box at the upper right.

> 4. When the desired item appears, tap **Buy** to download the book or periodical, or tap **Try a Sample** to download the start of the book for free.

Once you purchase an item, it is stored in your own library in the Amazon Cloud, and you can download it to your Fire as well as any other Kindles that you may own. You can also read your purchases using any of the free Kindle Reader Apps available for most personal computers and smartphones.

Buying or renting movies or TV shows

The hassle-free way to purchase or rent movies or TV shows and watch them on your Fire is to do so using Amazon's Video store, since it is so tightly integrated with the device. You can rent videos, in which case you get to watch the video for a specified time period. (The clock doesn't begin ticking until you first begin watching the video.) Alternately, you can purchase a video, in which case you can watch it whenever you like. There are just three simple steps involved in choosing and watching a video from Amazon's Video Store on your Fire:

> 1. At the Home screen, tap **Videos**.
>
> 2. In the Search box, enter your video's title, **OR** swipe out from the screen's left edge to browse the Video store.
>
> 3. When you find the video you want, tap **Rent** or **Buy**.

For most videos, you will see an option to purchase either standard definition or high definition. The cost of the rental or purchase gets charged to your 1-click billing account at Amazon.

NOTE: **Your video experience will be unacceptable without a high-speed internet connection.** Viewing movies or TV shows on your Fire (or on any tablet computer) requires the availability of a high-speed internet connection. If your internet speed is slow, you will see noticeable lags in your video playback. Your home network should be providing at least 2 MB of download speed for standard definition, and 4 MB of download speed for high-definition video. If you are sufficiently fortunate to own one of the newer ultra-high definition TV sets, you are looking at a minimum of 15 MB of continuous download speed for streaming. (You can test your network's speed by going to a free speed testing site, such as www.speedtest.net.) Also, be aware that **each device** on a home network adds to the streaming workload. You may think that your ten-megabit high-speed connection from your local cable company should suffice. However, if two parents have an iPad and a Fire HDX, four kids have their own Fire H6 tablets, two of the neighbors' kids who are visiting have their own tablets and all eight devices are streaming from the same network at the same time, the network is badly overloaded.

TIP **Serious videophile? Consider Amazon Prime and / or Netflix.** If you are a major fan of watching movies and television shows, the author has two recommendations for you. The first is that you seriously consider becoming a member of Amazon Prime. For an annual fee of under $100 (at the time of this writing), in addition to the free two day shipping on a variety of items, you will also get to watch thousands of movies and shows from the Amazon Prime video library at no cost. Prime members can also stream movies and TV shows. The second recommendation is that you seriously consider a subscription to Netflix. You can then download the Netflix app at no cost from the Amazon AppStore, log into your Netflix account, and enjoy any one of the thousands of movies and shows available on Netflix.

Buying music from Amazon's Music Store

You can browse, shop for, and purchase your favorite music hits and download music from Amazon's Music Store using your Fire; the following three steps are all that's necessary. (If you're outside the United States, see the note at the end of this section.)

1. At the Home screen, tap **Music**, and then tap **Store**.

2. In the Search box, enter your song or album title, **OR** swipe out from the screen's left edge to browse the Music store.

TIP **Narrow your search to quickly find what you are looking for.** You can narrow your search by swiping out from the left side of the screen and then tapping Bestsellers, New Releases, or Browse Genres.

3. When you locate the desired song or album, tap the button that displays the price, and confirm your purchase by tapping the Buy button. (In some cases, the songs are free, and if that is the case you will see a Get button. You can tap this button to get the song.)

TIP **Try before you buy.** If you want to listen to a sample of a song before purchasing the song, tap the 'Play' link (a triangle within a circle) beside the song's title. You'll hear a 30 second sample of the song.

Once you purchase a song or music album, it is in your account in the Amazon Cloud. You can download a song to your Fire at any time, by going to your Home page, tapping Music, tapping Cloud, and locating the desired song or album. Do a long-press (press and hold) on the song title or album cover until a popup menu appears, then choose 'Download' from the popup menu to download the song to your device.

NOTE: Copyright laws regarding music very from nation to nation. In order to buy music from Amazon's US-based Music store, you must have an Amazon account, a United States billing address, and a 1-click payment method that's been issued by a U.S. bank. And if you're using an Amazon gift card to make purchases, you must be physically located in the United States to use the Amazon Music Store. Amazon customers located within the United Kingdom can access the UK based Music store by going to www.amazon.co.uk and clicking the Music link.

Removing content from your device

If you are done with a particular book, magazine, or video, you can remove the item from your Fire. Use these steps to remove an item from your Fire:

1. Press **Home**.

2. At the Home screen, perform a 'long press' on the icon for the item.

3. At the popup menu that appears, choose **'Remove from Device**.'

The item remains in your personal space within the Amazon cloud, so you can always download the same item at a later time if you would like to again view the content.

Chapter 4: Free Books, Movies, and Music for your Fire

Your Fire is a great source of reading and entertainment, but let's face it: content costs, and quality contents costs more. Like everyone else, authors and songwriters certainly expect to eat (no surprise there), and production costs skyrocket when you get into the league of big-name entertainers and the costs of producing those Hollywood blockbusters that you're fond of watching on the 'small screen'. But there are great sources of free, quality content available for your Fire.

Easily Search the Kindle Store for Free Books

A great way to find free books is to search for… free books! As part of regular ongoing promotions, many authors will place their books on sale for nothing during certain days of a 90-day period, as part of an authors' program called Amazon KDP Select. You can take advantage of this fact by simply searching among any desired genre of Kindle books, and entering "0.00" as your search criteria in the Search box. What appears will be every Kindle book that has a price of zero dollars, zero cents on that particular day. (And before you think that checking this list would result in a limited selection, you should know that on any given day there are hundreds of free books offered through Amazon's promotional program.) This list of books will change wildly on a daily basis, so if you're an avid reader, you may find it worth your while to perform this sort of a search on a regular basis.

Getting Kindle Books from your local library (without setting foot in your library)

Many Kindle owners are oblivious to the fact that most public libraries now loan books, movies, music, and other digital content for the Amazon Kindle line of e-readers (as well as for other digital products like smartphones, Apple iPads, and other tablet computers.) In the United States alone, at the time of this writing, nearly 20,000 public libraries are members of a system called OverDrive Media. OverDrive Media provides an app for your Fire tablet that lets you borrow content electronically from your public library. All you'll need is the app (a free download from the Amazon store) and your library card number. Check with your local library to see if they are a member of the OverDrive program. You should be able to check without getting out of your easy chair; do a Google search for your town's public library web site, and once you find it, look for a link that says "download e-books" or something similar. If your city does not have a membership in such a program, there are libraries that allow nonresidents to obtain a library card for an annual fee. Two, at the time of this writing, are those of Fairfax County, Virginia (www.fairfaxcounty.gov/library for more information) and the City of Philadelphia (www.freelibrary.org for more information).

Once you've found that your library is a member of the OverDrive Media service, go to the Amazon App store, search on the term 'overdrive', and download the app to your Fire. Launch the app, and you'll be asked for a ZIP code; enter your zip code, and you'll see your local library's name in a list. Select your library by name, and you'll be taken to a page for your local library, where you can borrow books, movies, and other digital content. Browse among what your library has available for lending, click on a title, and you'll be taken to an Amazon page with the book, but in place of the "Buy with one click" button, you'll see a "Borrow from library" button. Click that button, and the book will be downloaded to your Fire.

Different libraries have different lending policies, so you'll want to check with your local library to determine the exact length of your loan. In my resident town of Charlotte, North Carolina, books have a two-week loan with one possible renewal, and movies are good for ten days. Many libraries now offer regularly scheduled classes or workshops that teach library patrons how to download digital content, so you may want to visit your local library and sign up for such a class in your home town.

Using the Kindle Owner's Lending Library ("KOLL") to your advantage

A second great free source of books is Amazon's own Kindle Owners Lending Library. If you are a member of Amazon Prime, you owe it to yourself to check out the Kindle Owners' Lending Library. The Kindle Owners Lending Library allows Amazon Prime members to borrow one book at a time each month, at no cost. There are thousands of books available through the service, and you can find free books to borrow through the Kindle Owners Lending Library using these steps:

1. At the Kindle Fire store, tap "**See all categories**." When the list of various categories (Books, Kindle Singles, Kindle Newsstand, New & Noteworthy, etc.) appears, tap the **Kindle Owners' Lending Library** option.

2. After picking the Kindle Owners' Lending Library, you can browse a list of books to borrow. You will know that a book is eligible for borrowing because it will have a "Prime" badge attached.

3. Click the '**Borrow**' tab. Next, you'll see a "Buy for $xx.xx" tab and a "Borrow for Free" tab. Click the "**Borrow for Free**" tab, and your borrowed book will be downloaded to your Fire.

TIP **Download free books from the Internet, and transfer these to your Fire using your USB cable.** The final source of free books that this chapter will detail is that of the Internet itself. You can find countless sources of free e-books on the Internet. These come in a variety of file formats; besides its own native file format of Kindle (.azw) files, your Fire will also read books in Adobe

Acrobat (.PDF) format, in MobiPocket (.MOBI) format, or in plain text (.TXT) format. Unfortunately, your Fire will NOT read files in the popular E-PUB format used by the Sony e-reader, the Barnes and Noble NOOK, and many other e-readers. The solution for this is not overwhelmingly complex; you can download free e-book converter programs that will convert e-books from most other formats into Amazon's Kindle (.KZW) format. An excellent program is called Calibre (go to www.calibre-ebook.com for details). Calibre can convert files from many formats, including the E-PUB format, into the Amazon Kindle file format. Once you convert the file, use the file transfer techniques described in Chapter 5 of this book, to transfer the e-books that you've converted to your Fire.

As for sources, performing a Google search for "free e-books" will return an avalanche of sites. Here is a small list to get you started:

Project Gutenberg- www.gutenberg.org

ManyBooks.net- http://manybooks.net

Google Books- http://books.google.com/

MobiPocket Free Books- www.mobipocket.com/freebooks/

An exhaustive source of free computer-based books can be found at http://freecomputerbooks.com. Finally, you'll find a surprisingly comprehensive list of textbooks that can be legally shared, at http://textbookrevolution.org. These are in .PDF format.

Free movies and TV shows with your Prime membership

If you are a major fan of watching movies and television shows or you are a fan of streaming music, the author has a recommendation for you. Consider becoming a member of Amazon Prime, if you aren't already a member. For an annual fee of under $100 (at the time of this writing), in addition to the free two day shipping on a variety of items, you will also get to watch thousands of movies and shows from the Amazon Prime video library on your Fire at no cost. Prime members can stream from a selection of thousands of movies and shows.

Your yearly subscription to Amazon Prime includes free unlimited access to thousands of movies and TV shows from Amazon Prime Instant Video, part of Amazon's own video streaming service. Note that there is Amazon Prime Instant Video and there is Amazon Instant Video, and the two aren't exactly the same. Amazon Instant Video is Amazon's video streaming service, with tens of thousands of movies and TV shows available for rent or purchase at various prices. Amazon Prime Instant Video is the library of all Amazon Instant Video content that happens to be free to Amazon Prime members. You can tell whether a video is free with your Prime membership by looking for the "Prime" banner at the upper-left corner, as shown in the following example:

To quickly browse what's available when you're a Prime member, at the Home Screen, tap 'Videos' in the main menu, then navigate to and tap a Prime-related subcategory— Recently Added to Prime, Top Movies in Prime Instant Videos, or Kids Movies in Prime Instant Videos (for movies), or Top TV in Prime Instant Videos and Kids TV in Prime Instant Videos (for TV shows). Once you have a subcategory selected, you can swipe left or right to locate a desired movie or show within that category, and tap the movie or TV show to begin watching.

Getting free music with Prime Music

When you are a Prime subscriber, you also receive the benefit of no-cost access to Amazon Prime Music. With Amazon Prime Music, you can listen to your choice of songs from a library of over one million songs. You can choose individual songs, entire albums, or customized playlists created by Amazon's music experts. You can also create your own playlists, and best of all, you can download songs of your choosing to your Fire so that you can listen later, even when you are off-line.

To get to Prime Music, go to the Home screen, and then tap "Music" in the menu bar. At the next screen that appears, tap Prime Music. This will take you to the Prime Music screen, shown here:

To listen to songs from Prime Music, at the Home screen, tap Music to navigate to your music library and browse or search by playlists, artists, albums, songs, or genres. Choose a song, album, or playlist and tap Play to begin playing the song, album, or playlist.

Creating a playlist

You can create playlists that contain your favorite songs using the following steps:

> 1. Click the check boxes next to the songs you want to add to the playlist.
>
> 2. Click "Add to playlist."
>
> 3. Click "New playlist" from the drop-down list that appears on the screen to create a new playlist.

Downloading Prime Music for Offline Playback

On any Amazon Fire, as well as phones and other tablets with the Amazon Music app installed, Prime members can also download Prime Music (including Prime Playlists) for offline playback. You can use these steps to download Prime Music for offline playback:

> 1. Add the Prime Music you want to download to your music library.
>
> 2. Search or browse your music library for the Prime song, album, or playlist you want to download.
>
> 3. On a Fire or on an Android tablet, press and hold the title you want to download, and then choose Download from the menu that appears. On an Apple iPad or iPhone, swipe the songs you want to download, tap More, and then tap Download.

You can find the offline versions in the Prime Playlists section under the Playlist view in your music library.

Licensing Limitations of Prime Music

Prime Music is available for streaming on only one device at a time, for each Amazon account. Prime Music is available to download (for offline playback) to only four devices at a time, for each Amazon account. If you try to download Prime Music to an additional device, you will be asked to (1)-start the download on that device (and automatically deactivate the Prime Music that you downloaded to your least recently used device), or (2)-leave your active device settings unchanged. Finally, due to music licensing agreements, Prime Music is (at the time of this writing) limited to Amazon customers having a US or Puerto Rico mailing address, with the account billed to a financial institution based in the US or Puerto Rico.

Have music, will travel...

Keep in mind that your Fire isn't the only way in which you can enjoy Prime music. In addition to using your Fire, you can also use the Amazon Music App on any compatible platform. The Amazon Music App is available for nearly all Android phones and tablets, and Apple iOS devices including the iPhone and iPad lines. To download the app, go to the respective app store for your device (such as the Google PlayStore for an Android phone), and search on the term "Amazon music app."

Chapter 5: Surfing the Web with the Silk Browser

The Amazon Silk web browser for the Fire is unique among web browsers, engineered from the ground up especially for the Fire. Since Android-based tablets will certainly run established browsers such as Google Chrome and Mozilla Firefox, many have wondered why Amazon chose to design a new browser from scratch. The answer is, Amazon wanted to offer a fast browsing experience, so the browser design splits tasks between the browser software that is running locally on the Fire, and Amazon's Cloud Servers. As a result of this unique design, a number of features are familiar to you because you've seen them in other browsers, but there are a few that are unique to the Silk browser.

Check out the Amazon Help Video.

Amazon has taken the time to provide a short help video about the Silk browser. You can view the video at the Amazon web site. Point a web browser at www.amazon.com/help and at the page that appears, click "Fire, Kindle and Echo" on the left, then click "Fire HD and HDX Tablets" on the right. At the next page, under "Getting Started," click "Fire Tablet Help Videos," then click "Using the Silk Browser."

Starting the Silk Browser

To launch the Silk browser, at the Home screen, finger-swipe the Navigation bar near the top to the far right and tap Web, or tap the Silk Browser icon within the carousel (it resembles the following):

Silk browser

. Tap the icon or tap Web' in the Navigation bar, and (assuming you have an active Internet connection) the Silk browser opens to the web page for the last site you visited. The following illustration shows the parts of the Silk browser.

The Silk browser is a tabbed browser, like Google's Chrome, Mozilla Firefox, and more recent versions of Microsoft Internet Explorer. To open a new tab, just tap the plus sign in the top right corner. You can then tap in the Search field and enter the desired web address.

Quick access to the Quick Menu

The Silk browser has a number of options and settings that can be reached from the Quick menu. And with the Fire HD7 and HD6 models comes a new way to get there. If you press and swipe from the left edge off the device (just outside the visible screen area) out to the right, you will drag open the Silk browser's Quick menu, shown in the following illustration. (You can also tap the three horizontal lines at the upper-left corner.)

From here, you can access your bookmarks, history of recently-visited pages, downloads, and pages that are "trending now" across the web. You can also access the Settings page which offers various ways to customize the settings of the Silk browser, as explained in later parts of this chapter.

TIP **If you are viewing a page and there is a link embedded in the page and you would like to go**

to that link in a separate tab, give the link a long press rather than a tap. A menu of options will appear, and you can choose 'Open in new tab' from the menu.

TIP **Share web pages with your friends.**
When a page is displayed in the Silk browser, the Quick menu icon (three vertical dots) at the bottom of the browser window will include a Share Page symbol. Tap this symbol, and you can send a link to the page either via email, or through Facebook or Twitter.

TIP **The "thumb and finger spread" or "thumb and finger pinch" works in the Silk browser.**
You will often encounter web pages with text that is too small to read on the Fire screen. Place your thumb and finger on the screen and spread them to magnify, or pinch them together to reduce the magnification.

TIP **Use "Find on this page" as a search tool.** Oftentimes you will need to search a website for a particular word or phrase. To do this in the Silk browser, tap the quick menu icon (three vertical dots) at the bottom of the window, then tap "Find in page." Enter a search term in the search field that appears, and use the up and down arrow keys to move through the search results.

TIP **Let the browser complete your entry.**
As you begin typing characters into the search / address field, a list of suggestions appears below the field. Type more characters, and suggestions increase in accuracy. When you see a suggestion that matches the URL you intended to type, tap that suggestion.

Using Bookmarks

As with all modern web browsers, the Silk browser provides the ability to bookmark sites so that you can easily return to the same site. Use these steps to add a bookmark:

1. Tap the Quick Menu icon at the bottom of the browser window.

2. Tap **Add Bookmark**. You will now see the Add Bookmarks dialog box.

3. Change the name of the entry to something friendlier if you desire.

4. Tap **OK**, to add the page to your bookmarked pages.

There are different ways to go to a bookmarked page, but this method seems to involve the least amount of steps.

1. Press at the left edge of the screen and swipe to the right, to drag the Silk sidebar out.

2. Tap **Bookmarks**.

3. Locate the desired bookmark.

4. Tap the desired bookmark to open it in the current page.

You can also perform a long press on the desired bookmark, and choose Open in New Tab from the menu that appears to open the webpage in a new tab.

TIP **Delete any bookmark page that's no longer needed.** From the Bookmarks page (get there by tapping the Menu icon at the top left, or by pressing and swiping out from the left edge of the screen, and tapping Bookmarks), perform a long-press on the unwanted bookmark, and choose "Delete" from the menu that appears.

Changing Silk Settings for Best Operation

You will likely wish to choose your preferred search engine. The default search engine for the Silk browser is Microsoft Bing, but if you prefer to use Google or Yahoo as your default search engine, you can change the Silk browser to either of these options. Tap the menu icon at the upper left corner or press at the left edge and swipe outwards, tap Settings, tap Search Engine, and make your desired choice.

TIP **Keep Silk performance up through regular housecleaning**. Just as browsers on your PC can be slowed over time from too many cookies or from a clogged cache, so can the Silk browser. You can perform a bit of browser housecleaning on occasion; to do so, tap the menu icon at the upper left corner or press at the left edge and swipe outwards, tap Settings, and tap the Clear Browser Data option.

The Silk browser has a number of settings that you can use to change the operation of the browser. Tap the menu icon at the upper left corner or press at the left edge and swipe outwards, and then tap Settings. You will see the settings that apply to the browser, as shown in the following illustration.

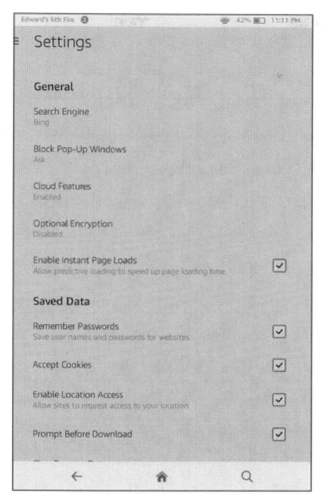

(Silk browser settings)

These settings affect the way the Silk Browser behaves in various ways. Under Search Engine, you can specify the desired search engine used by the browser, and you can choose to block popup windows and whether to enable cloud-based features of the Amazon Cloud. The Enable Instant Page Loads option is by default set to on; however you may wish to consider turning off this option if the types of websites that you visit appear to be hampered by predictive page loading.

If you scroll down in the Silk Settings screen, you will see additional options revealed, as shown in the following illustration.

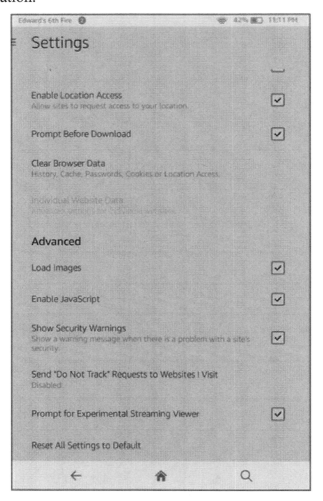

These options include whether or not you want to clear browser data (the history, the cache, and all cookie data) from the browser. You also have options to remember passwords used when visiting sites, to clear all passwords from the browser memory, and whether or not cookies should be accepted by the browser. You can enable location tracking or clear location access, and under Advanced Settings, you can

72

choose whether images are normally loaded, whether JavaScript is enabled, and whether security warnings are enabled.

Chapter 6: Adding Content by Moving and Copying Files

In press reviews, the Amazon Fire product line has taken a fair share of criticism for being a relatively "closed ecosystem," according to its critics. Many reviewers have claimed that Fire owners are dependent on purchasing virtually all content from Amazon. In the opinion of this author, that reputation is somewhat undeserved. Certainly, it is in Amazon's interest to get you to buy your content from Amazon. But the 'closed ecosystem' claim made by many members of the press implies that you must purchase all your content from Amazon, and that is simply not the case. In addition to purchasing content from the Amazon store, you can find millions (literally!) of books from other sources, and these can be copied to your Fire from your computer using the USB cable that is a part of your charging assembly. The Fire uses the .mobi file format for its e-books, and e-books in the .mobi format can be found in thousands of places all over the internet, some paid, and others free. There are also millions of books in the popular E-PUB format used by Sony and by Google, and there are free converters readily available from hundreds of sources on the web that will convert files from the E-PUB format into the .mobi format used by all Amazon Kindles.

You can use the same USB cable techniques to copy MP3, AAC, or WAV files that you obtain from your own sources, and these become a part of the music library on your Fire. There are apps like Crackle that let you stream any one of thousands of free movies or TV shows to your Fire. If you are already a Netflix subscriber, you can download the Netflix app from the Amazon app store (the app is free) and watch any content that you would normally obtain from Netflix on your Fire. And short length, personal movies compatible with the

Fire (in 3gp or mp4 format) can also be copied to the device, although the 8 gigabyte memory size is by nature going to limit the length of movies that can be stored locally on the device. (By comparison, an average Blu-ray DVD occupies 25 gigabytes of disk space.)

You can also email documents directly to your Fire, using Amazon's free Send to Kindle service. Every registered Kindle has its own assigned email address, and you can send certain types of files- Microsoft Word documents, rich text (RTF) or text (TXT) files, .JPG or .PNG graphics files, Adobe PDF files, and others- to your Fire's assigned email address. (See the following heading if you do not know your Fire's assigned e-mail address.) Within roughly 5 minutes of the time that you send a file as an attachment, it will show up on your Fire, in the Documents folder. You can then tap the document to open it and read it in the native Kindle Viewer, and there are apps available that will let you edit Microsoft Word documents on your Kindle.

To take full advantage of all of these features of the Fire, you'll need to know how to use the file management features of the Fire. You'll find the various tips, tricks, and traps that pertain to these topics covered throughout this chapter.

Check out the Amazon Help Video.

Amazon has taken the time to provide a short help video on the subject of moving files between a computer and your Fire. You can view the video at the Amazon web site. Point a web browser at www.amazon.com/help and at the page that appears, click "Fire, Kindle and Echo" on the left, then click "Fire HD and HDX Tablets" on the right. At the next page, under "Getting Started," click "Fire Tablet Help Videos," then click "Transferring content from your computer."

Sending Files to your Fire via E-mail

If you purchased your Fire directly from Amazon, it was registered for you when it arrived. If you purchased it from a retailer such as Best Buy, you may have gone through the setup steps on your own. In either case, your Fire has been assigned a Send to Kindle email address. This address is something similar to ***username@kindle.com***. To see your email address, pull down the Navigation bar, tap Settings, and under Settings, tap My Account. You will see a message that reads something like-

Edward's second Kindle is registered to Edward Jones

edjones45@kindle.com

This is the email address that you can use to send files as attachments to your Fire.

***WARNING*: Before you can send any documents to your Fire, you must add the sending email address to an "Approved personal document email list" under your Amazon account settings**. To prevent Fire owners from receiving unwanted spam, Amazon blocks any email sent to any address at Kindle.com that hasn't been added to the approved personal document email list. Log into your Amazon account in a computer's web browser, and under the 'Your Account' link, click 'Manage Your Devices.' At the next screen that appears, you'll see all your Amazon devices (assuming you own more than one). If you own just one Fire, you will see just that device. Scroll down and locate the desired Fire in your list of devices, click the Edit link to the right of the device name, and you will be able to change the e-mail address registered to that Kindle. You can also add authorized e-mail addresses that will be permitted to send e-mail to your Kindle. By default, Amazon adds the e-mail address that is associated with your Amazon account. To add authorized addresses, under 'Your Account' at the left, click Personal Document Settings, then look for the Approved Personal Document E-mail List near the bottom of the screen. You can click the 'Add a new Approved E-mail Address' link in this area to add another email address.

Once you've added your email address to the approved personal document email list, you can attach files to an email message and send it to your send to kindle address. Documents can be in the form of .DOC, .DOCX, .RTF, .TXT, .HTM or .HTML, ZIP, .MOBI' and .AZW file formats. Images can be sent in the .JPG, .PNG, .GIF, or .BMP file formats. The conversion process assumes an active wi-fi connection, since Amazon's Send to Kindle service converts your file into Amazon's own .AZW file format, then downloads it to your Fire using Amazon's Whispernet.

WARNING: **Attachments cannot be larger than 50 megabytes per attachment, and each email must not have more than 25 attachments.** If any of your files are larger than 50 megabytes, the Send to Kindle process will fail for that file, and that file will not appear in your Documents folder.

TIP **Use the Send to Kindle service to convert PDF files to Amazon readable documents**. In addition to the file types listed in the previous tip, you can also send PDF files to your Kindle, and Amazon uses a conversion service to convert the PDF file into Amazon's own .AZW file format. Simply add the word "convert" to the subject line of your email, then attach the PDF file and send the email to your Send to Kindle email address.

Transferring Files to your Fire with its Charging Cable

You can also transfer files from a laptop or desktop computer to your Fire, using a USB to micro-USB cable. This is the same type of cable that is supplied as a charging cable for your Fire; one end contains the micro USB connector that plugs into the base of your Fire, and the other end contains a standard USB connector. Use the cable to connect your Fire to your computer, and the Fire will appear as a USB flash drive under your computer's operating system.

NOTE: **Users of Windows XP may have to install additional software before using a USB cable to access the Fire, and the users of the Apple Mac will have to install additional software.** Go to the following link for additional details:

`http://www.kindle.com/support/downloads`

Once the Fire appears as a USB drive under your computer's operating system, you can simply drag and drop or copy and paste the desired files into the appropriate folders of the Fire.

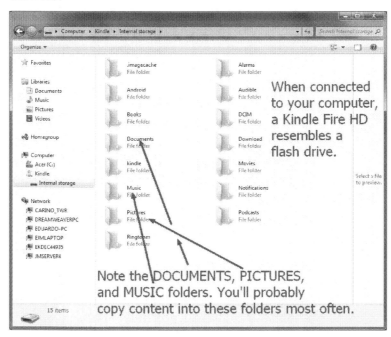

You can use a USB cable to transfer files in the form of .DOC, .DOCX, .XLS, .PPT, .RTF, .TXT, .HTM or .HTML, ZIP, .MOBI' and .AZW file formats. Images can be in the

.JPG, .PNG, .GIF, or .BMP file formats, and audio files can be in the .AAC, .MP3, .MIDI, .OGG, or .WAV file formats.

TIP **If you transfer files that have been saved in the common Microsoft office formats, you can edit these files on your Fire tablet.** Fire tablets include WPS Office, a popular Android app that lets you view, edit, and save files in the Microsoft Word, Excel, and PowerPoint formats. If you don't see the app on your Apps screen, tap the Search icon on your Home screen and search for "WPS Free Mobile Office." There are additional third-party apps available at various prices, including Kingsoft Office by Kingsoft, and Documents to Go by DataWiz.

Transferring Files Wirelessly with Wi-Fi File Explorer

You can transfer files to your Fire wirelessly ('look ma, no cables!') Assuming you have a home network with PCs attached to it, you don't necessarily have to resort to the annoyance of a cable connected between your Fire and your computer every time you want to move a file between the two. Wi-Fi File Explorer is a neat little app that lets you transfer files wirelessly. Download and install this free app on your Fire, and when you run the app, once you identify the wi-fi network used by the Fire, you'll see a display giving you a web address that you can point a browser on any computer that's also on your network. The address will include a port number, similar to the following:

http://192.168.1.15:8000

Point your computer's web browser to the address you're given (yours will likely differ from this example) and you'll see a display like the following:

Wi-Fi File Explorer gives you a file explorer view of all the folders on your Fire. You can drill down into any folder, and use the Download button at the top of the Wi-Fi File Explorer window to move files from your laptop to your Fire, without the hassle of wires.

Chapter 7: Fire Email, Contacts, and Calendar

One of the many capabilities of the Fire centers on the email client that is built into the device. All of the basic features that you would expect to find in an email client are here; you can open and read mail, reply to and compose mail, download attachments, and send email with attached files. The HD6 and HD7 models of the Fire add significant improvements to the built-in e-mail client. Clearly Amazon engineering has been paying attention to user feedback, because the e-mail client that was mediocre at best in the first generation Fires has improved to a level of capable, in this author's opinion. The e-mail app now supports labeling, threaded conversations, and archiving of emails for offline reading. Integrated calendar support of both Google's Gmail and Microsoft Exchange are additional welcome features.

Check out the Amazon Help Video.

Amazon has taken the time to provide a short help video on the subject of e-mail. You can view the video at the Amazon web site. Point a web browser at www.amazon.com/help and at the page that appears, click "Fire, Kindle and Echo" on the left, then click "Fire HD and HDX Tablets" on the right. At the next page, under "Getting Started," click "Fire Tablet Help Videos," then click "E-mail, calendar, and contacts."

You can set up most email accounts quickly with Auto-configuration. If you're like many individuals, you probably have a number of e-mail accounts. With your Fire, you can stay on top of your e-mail from anywhere. Later sections of this chapter will delve into using e-mail on the Fire in greater detail, but for now, you may find the great auto-configuration feature is all you need to get your multiple e-mail accounts up and running. The feature works with e-mail accounts provided by Google (Gmail), Yahoo Mail, AOL Mail, Microsoft Live Mail (formerly known as Hotmail), Microsoft's Outlook.com, Apple's iCloud Mail, and BT Internet (United Kingdom). Use the following steps to set up your e-mail account on your Fire:

1. From the Home 🏠 screen, tap Apps in the Navigation bar.

2. Tap '**Device**' at the upper right to see the apps on your device,

3. Tap the Email app icon (shown here).

Mail icon in Carousel

Mail icon in Favorites

Assuming you've never setup an email account on your Fire, the Add Account screen will appear, as shown in the following illustration. (If an e-mail account has been set up on your device and you want to add another, drag down the Navigation bar from the top of the screen, and tap Settings > Applications >Email, Contacts, Calendar > Add Account.)

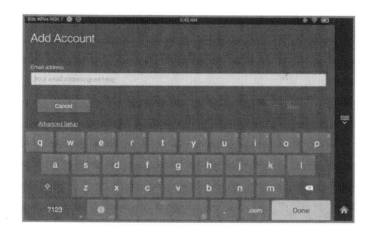

Enter your e-mail address and then tap Next. You may now see a sign-in screen for Google, Yahoo, AOL, Microsoft Live or Outlook Mail, or iCloud, depending on your choice of e-mail providers, or you may see a screen asking for your password. (An example of the sign-in screen presented to users of Google's Gmail is shown in the following illustration.)

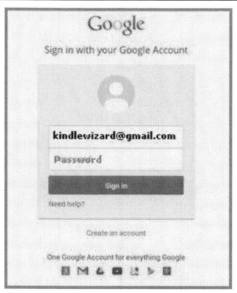

Enter any requested information, and your Fire will attempt to connect the new email account settings with the servers of your email account provider. Once it successfully does so, you'll see a synchronization options screen, similar to the one shown in the following illustration:

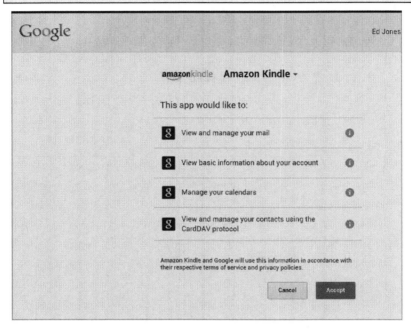

This screen asks for permission to synchronize your contacts and calendar on your Fire with that of your e-mail provider. Tap Accept, and in a moment, you should see a screen indicating a successful setup of your e-mail account.

TIP **Fire receives incoming emails, but is unable to send outgoing emails.** After setup of an email account, some users report that they are able to receive emails, but can't send mail. The problem is usually that when you fill in the setup screen, the Fire assumes that your username is also your outgoing SMTP address setting. And this is true with most providers, but not with all providers. As an example, if your email provider is Comcast cable, and your full email address is *johndoe@comcast.net*, when going through the setup screen, you probably entered *johndoe* when prompted for a user name. As a result, the Fire's email client is trying to send out email with an SMTP address setting of *johndoe*, when the setting should be *johndoe@comcast.net*. To solve the problem, go back into the email settings you have on your Fire, and enter the entire outgoing email address manually. (For details on how to do this, see the following topic.)

Setting up e-mail manually

The automated e-mail setup on the Fire does a great job when it works, but it does not always work, and when it fails to work, you'll need to set up your e-mail manually. Before starting a manual e-mail account setup process, there is some information that you will want to make sure that you have from your e-mail service provider. Of course, you will need to know your e-mail address and the password for the account. In addition, you will need to know the server settings of your mail server. You will need the SMTP settings, as well as either the POP or the IMAP settings. (The SMTP setting is used for sending mail, and POP and IMAP are both used for receiving mail. IMAP is a newer standard for receiving mail, so if your mail server supports both POP and IMAP, use the IMAP settings.) Finally, you will need to know the security type used by the servers, and the default incoming and outgoing ports. (You should be able to obtain all of this information from your e-mail provider.) Once you've obtained the information, perform the following steps to manually set up an e-mail account on the Fire:

1. If no e-mail accounts currently exist on your device, tap Apps, then tap the E-mail icon.

2. At the next screen, tap Create E-mail account. If one or more e-mail accounts already exist on your device,

drag down the Navigation bar and tap Settings, and then tap Applications > Email, Contacts, Calendar.

3. At the next screen that appears, tap Add Account.

4. Enter your e-mail address and password where prompted, and then tap Next. You will see an Add Account screen asking you to choose the type of account, as shown in the following illustration.

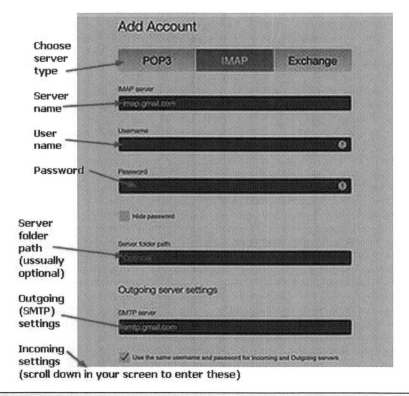

5. Select the type of email account you are creating. (Your available choices are a POP3 account, an IMAP account, or a Microsoft Exchange Account. The remainder of this topic will help you with the common POP3 and IMAP types; if you are setting up a Microsoft Exchange-hosted account, see the following topic for details.

6. Next, you will be asked to provide your incoming server settings. These will include your user name, password, POP3 or IMAP server address, security type, port number, and the desired 'delete email from server' setting. Enter this information, then tap Done at the bottom of the screen.

Your Fire will attempt to connect to the Incoming server with the settings you supplied. If the connection is successful, the Outgoing server settings screen will appear.

7. Enter your outgoing server settings. These will include your user name, password, SMTP server address, security type (if any), port number, and whether the server will require a sign-in. After entering this information, tap Next.

8. The first time you connect, you will be asked to give this mail account a unique on-screen name, and you will need to supply your name. (The e-mail app uses the unique account name to differentiate the account from all other email accounts on your Fire.) Touch Done, and your manually created e-mail account is ready for use.

NOTE: Manual setups of e-mail accounts can be tricky, to say the least. You are required to enter a number of values, and if any single value is incorrect, your e-mail works partially, or does no work at all. If you are unsuccessful in setting up your e-mail account, try changing the entry in the 'username' field to your full e-mail address. Some systems expect to see your full e-mail address (such as 'johndoe@carolinarr.timewarnercable.com'), and other systems only want to see the username ('such as 'johndoe'). If you've tried both formats with no success, it's probably time to get as many details about the settings as possible from your e-mail provider, and then punch that 'Help' button on your Fire, and find the current phone number for Amazon technical support.

Setting up E-mail with Microsoft Exchange

In the business world, one of the most commonly-used sources of e-mail is Microsoft's Exchange, a server-based messaging system used by thousands of companies and organizations worldwide. Exchange is offered both as a hardware-and-software based solution that is typically installed and managed by an organization's IT staff, or as a cloud-based solution (as is the case with Microsoft's Office 365, a subscription-based service offered by Microsoft). In either case, if Microsoft Exchange is the provider of e-mail, contacts, and calendaring at your office, the good news is that you can set up your Fire to access your e-mail, contacts, and calendar that are hosted by Microsoft Exchange. The Fire sports major improvements to the operating system that make an Exchange e-mail account setup much simpler than on earlier generation Kindle Fires. You'll want to turn on your Fire and ensure that you have an active Wi-Fi connection. Once this is done, you can perform the following steps to set up e-mail, contacts, and calendaring from Microsoft Exchange on your Fire:

1. If no e-mail accounts currently exist on your device, tap Apps, then tap the E-mail icon, and when the next screen appears, tap Create E-mail account. If one or more e-mail accounts already exist on your device, drag down the Navigation bar and tap Settings, and then tap Applications > Email, Contacts, Calendar.

2. At the next screen that appears, tap Add Account.

3. Enter your e-mail address and password where prompted, and then click Done. You will now see an Add Account screen asking you to choose the type of account, as shown in the following illustration.

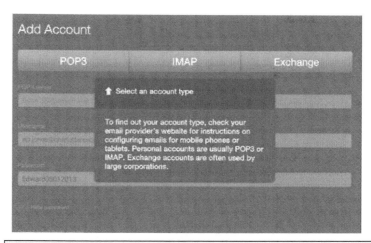

4. At the top of this screen, tap Exchange. The next screen that you see, shown in the following illustration, asks you for the settings that apply to your Microsoft Exchange server. These include the server name, your username and password on the Exchange server, the server's Domain name (often optional), and the security settings and ports used by the server.

5. In the Exchange server field, enter the name of your Exchange server. If you're connecting to a Microsoft cloud-based Office 365 email account, the Exchange server name will be **outlook.office365.com**. If you are using a web-hosted Exchange account provided by a

web hosting service like 1and1 Internet or GoDaddy.com, your hosting provider will be able to provide you with this information. If you're not using Office 365 or a web-hosted Exchange account, contact the Exchange server administrator at your organization's I.T. department for the name of your Exchange server.

6. Under Username, enter your full email address, and in the Password field, make sure your password is correct, then click Done.

7. The Domain field will contain the word, 'Optional.' Unless a domain name has been given to you by a web-based hosting provider or by your organization's I.T. department, you can leave this field empty.

8. If your web-based hosting provider or by your organization's I.T. department has provided you with security settings and /or port settings needed by your Exchange server, click the 'Security Settings and Ports' link beneath the 'Domain' field. This will result in the display of another screen, asking about secure connections (SSL) options and port settings. Enter the details given by your email provider, and click Save.

9. You may see a Remote security administration notice that reads, "The server <Your Exchange Server Name> requires that you allow it to remotely control some security features on your device. Do you want to finish setting up this account?" If this notice appears, tap OK.

10. Finally, you will see a screen bearing the descriptive name of your e-mail account, along with synchronization options for synchronizing your contacts and calendar on the Exchange server with the contacts and calendar on your Fire. Turn on the Contacts and Calendar checkboxes as desired, to specify whether or not you want to synchronize your contacts and calendar items between Microsoft Exchange and your Fire. After making your selections, tap Save. (Note that by default, your e-mail will be synchronized between the e-mail account on

the Fire and the e-mail account under Microsoft Exchange; you cannot turn off e-mail synchronization.)

After tapping Save, a 'Setup complete!' screen appears, and you can tap View Inbox to access your Exchange-based email on your Fire.

Reading your E-Mail

The e-mail client that is provided with your Fire does all that you would expect of a solid e-mail client. You can read, compose, and send emails, and you can add attachments to those emails. You can also read e-mails that contain attachments of many file types, including pictures, video attachments, Adobe .PDF attachments, and Microsoft office document attachments. The e-mail client also integrates with the Contacts app that is built into the Fire, so you can send e-mails to contacts that you enter in your contacts directory.

You perform most common mail-related tasks from your Inbox. To get to your Inbox, tap Apps, then locate and tap the Email icon, shown here.

Your Inbox opens, displaying your mail in a fashion similar to that shown here, assuming that you are in landscape view. (If you are in portrait view, you will only see either the message list or the contents of the message at one time, so you may want to switch to landscape view for best reading by rotating the Fire.)

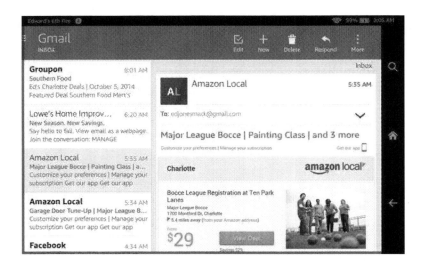

To read an e-mail, just open the Inbox, and tap the desired mail item in the list at the left to open the mail. When you do so, its content will appear in the active portion of the screen, at the right.

Switching between multiple mail accounts

If you've set up more than one e-mail account, you can switch by tapping the Menu icon (at the top left corner of the E-mail screen). An e-mail sidebar will open, and you can tap the inbox name for the account you want to check.

TIP The Fire e-mail app has a nice feature called the *combined inbox*, which displays mail from multiple accounts simultaneously (assuming that you have set up more than one e-mail account on your device). Tap the Menu icon (at the top left corner of the E-mail screen), and choose Combined Inbox from the sidebar that opens. Once you do this, you will see all messages from all established accounts within a single list.

94

Composing and Sending Mail

Writing email is also a straightforward process. Use these steps to compose a new e-mail:

At the Home screen tap Apps, then tap the E-Mail icon to get into the e-mail app. When your Inbox opens, note the toolbar that appears at the upper right, as shown in the following illustration.

Using the toolbar buttons, you can compose a new e-mail, reply to an e-mail, or delete an e-mail from your Inbox.

Once in the e-mail app, tap the New icon in the toolbar to display a New Message screen (shown here).

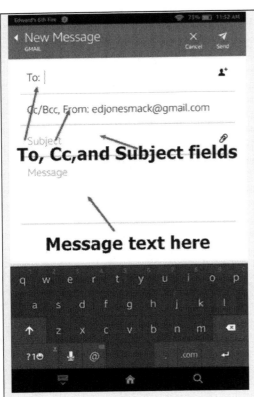

To, Cc, and Subject fields

Message text here

Enter the recipient's e-mail address in the To box. (Alternately, you can tap the Contacts icon and choose an address that's in your Contacts list.) When entering multiple names, separate any additional names with commas. (You can also use the Cc: and Bcc: fields to add copied recipients and blind copied recipients, respectively.)

In the Subject area, enter a subject for the message, and then enter the desired message text in the Message area. You can add attachments (such as photos stored on your Fire) by tapping the icon of a paper clip at the right side of the message. When you tap this icon, the menu shown here opens, and you can choose Attach a Photo, Attach File, or Capture a Photo from the menu. (If you choose Attach a Photo, you can select an image stored in the \Pictures folder of your Fire, while choosing

Attach File lets you select a file that is stored in your \Documents folder of your Fire. Choose Capture a Photo to take a photo using one of the built-in cameras of the Fire, and immediately send that photo as an attachment.

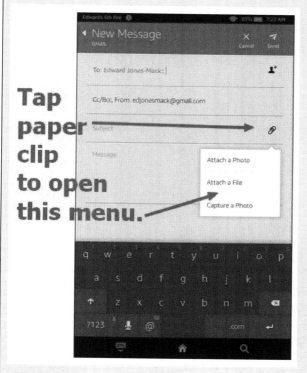

When done composing your message and adding any necessary attachments, tap the Send icon in the upper-right portion of the toolbar to send your message.

Customize your E-mail operation with various settings

Speed up your email performance by hiding images. If you receive a large amount of email that contains embedded images, display of your messages can be slowed by the presence of the images. You can turn off the display of embedded images by default. Pull down the Navigation bar, tap Settings, and under Applications, within the 'Amazon Applications' subcategory, tap 'Email, Contacts, Calendar. At the next screen that appears, tap Email Settings. You will a screen similar to the following:

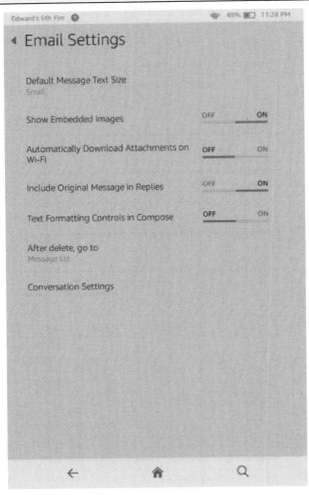

Show embedded images is normally on by default at this screen. Set this option to Off to speed up your mail performance.

TIP **Add a custom signature to save typing time**. You can add a default signature line to the bottom of your outgoing messages, to save yourself the time involved in having to sign every letter that you compose. To do this, drag down the Navigation bar and tap Settings, then at the Settings screen, tap Applications, then tap Email/Contacts/Calendar, and then tap Email Settings. At the next screen that appears select the desired email account by name, scroll down within the dialog box, tap Signature, and enter the desired personal signature.

TIP **Use Bulk delete to delete multiple messages**. There is no need to delete messages one at a time if you want to delete a group of messages. Just turn on the checkboxes at the left of all of the unwanted messages, and tap the Delete icon at the top of the screen to delete the selected messages as a group.

Using your synchronized calendars and contacts

Once you've set up your e-mail accounts, assuming that you allow synchronization of calendars and contacts with your e-mail accounts, you will also be able to use the Calendar and Contacts apps built into your Fire. At the Home screen, tap Apps, then tap Calendar. A view of a synchronized calendar from your Google, Microsoft, iCloud, or Yahoo account will appear (the illustration that follows shows an example of a synchronized calendar based on a Google account).

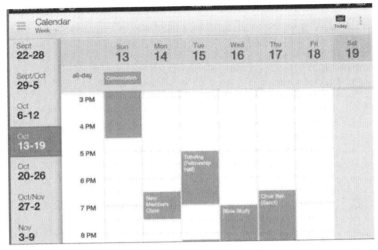

You can make changes or additions to your calendar by tapping within any date and time field, and then tapping the Plus (+) symbol that appears. A New Event screen will appear as shown in the following illustration, and you can enter the details about your calendar event.

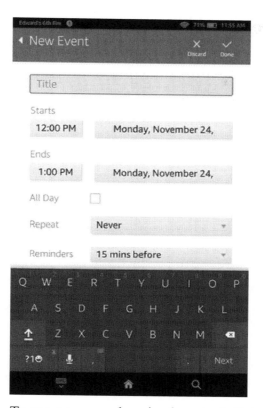

    To see your synchronized contacts list, get to the Home screen, tap Apps, and locate and tap the Contacts icon. A synchronized contacts list will appear; the following illustration shows an example of a Contacts list based on a Google account. (And yes, the author does have a fondness for dead presidents, particularly the ones depicted on greenbacks, but that is another story.)

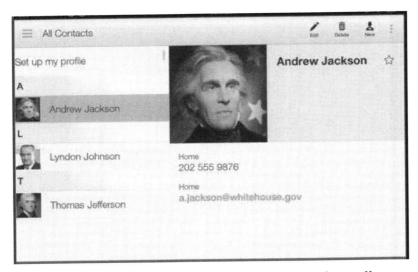

Set up my profile

A

Andrew Jackson

L

Lyndon Johnson

T

Thomas Jefferson

Andrew Jackson ☆

Home
202 555 9876

Home
a.jackson@whitehouse.gov

When viewing any contact, you can use the toolbar buttons that appear at the upper-right to edit an existing contact in your list, to delete a contact, or to add a new contact. As with the calendar, since the accounts are synchronized with those of your e-mail provider, any changes that you make using your Fire will be entered in the cloud-based contacts list provided by your e-mail provider.

Chapter 8: It's Your Life: Photos, Music, & Personal Videos

One of the major strengths of the Fire centers on its impressive multimedia capabilities. Designed to provide you with a better multimedia experience, the Fire HD6 and HD7 models are small enough to hold in your hand, yet deliver a vibrant viewing experience with over 16 million colors on their high definition screens. The HD7 provides stereo speakers built into the device while the HD6 provides a single mono speaker, and both models include a headphone jack. For the technically inclined, the Fire HD6 and HD7 support 3gp and mp4 video formats, H264 video encoding, with an 800 by 480 resolution and a 2500 kps bit rate. On the audio side, the Fire HD6 and HD7 support Dolby noise reduction, AAC, MP3, MIDI, OGG, and WAV formats, and use AAC for audio encoding of movies' audio tracks.

Playing personal videos on your Fire

You can transfer video files or download video files and play them on your Fire. You cannot place them in the video library, but you can copy your personal videos into the /Pictures subfolder of your Fire (and no, "/Pictures" is not a misprint). Your videos will appear alongside your photos when you tap Photos on the Navigation bar. The only visual difference between your photos and your videos will be the presence of an arrow within a circle, like this:

which acts as a "Play" button for the video player. Tap the arrow, and your video will begin playing on your Fire's screen.

You can copy files that are stored in the 3GP or MP4 video format into the /Pictures folder that appears in the directory of folders shown on your computer when the Fire is connected by means of the USB cable. When you connect the Fire to the micro USB side of the charging cable and connect the standard USB side of the cable to your computers USB port, the Fire appears on your computer's File Explorer or file management system as a USB flash drive, similar to the example shown in the following illustration.

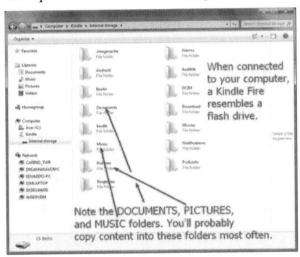

You can then use standard cut / copy / paste or drag-and-drop procedures to copy the video file from the source folder that contains the video file on your hard drive to the destination folder that appears with all the other folders of your Fire's internal storage under the device name 'Fire.'

You can copy your photos, images, or personal video files into the /Pictures folder, and these will appear within a tiled directory style view when you tap Photos in the Navigation bar on your Home screen. In a similar fashion, you can copy .mp3 files into the /Music subfolder, and these will appear as songs when you tap Music in the Navigation bar. You can copy Microsoft Word documents, rich text format (.RTF) files, and text (.TXT) files into the /Documents folder, and these will appear when you tap Documents in the Navigation bar.

WARNING: A file may exist in the acceptable file format of 3GP or MP4, yet may refuse to play on a Fire. Not only must the files be stored as a 3GP or MP4 format, the length by width (800 by 480) and video bitrate (2500) must fall within acceptable parameters, or the video will fail to play. You can use a conversion program on a desktop or laptop computer to convert video files such as your vacation movies shot with a DV camcorder to a format that will play on your Fire.

There is an excellent free, open source program for converting video files to the Fire format, and the program is available for the Windows PC, Apple Mac, and Ubuntu Linux machines. The program, Miro, can be downloaded at http://www.getmiro.com. The program may appear slightly complicated to use, at least initially. Fortunately, the getmiro.com website provides extensive documentation.

Importing your Music Library from other sources to your Fire

You can import your iTunes, Microsoft Zune, or other music library into your Fire using the Amazon Cloud Player. Amazon has an easy to use tool that makes importing your iTunes of other music library a simple matter. Open a browser window on your computer, and visit http://www.amazon.com/cloudplayer (if you are in North America) or visit http://www.amazon.co.uk/cloudplayer (if you are in the United Kingdom) and set up a CloudPlayer account. Once you set up an account, click the Import Music button at the upper left, and follow the directions that appear on the screen. After you've imported your songs into the Amazon Cloud Player, you can select any number of songs, click the download button, and download them to your Fire.

Downloading and playing YouTube videos

You can download YouTube videos for later playback on your Fire. YouTube has long supported the H.264 video encoding format that is currently used by the Fire. And if a subject has ever been recorded on video, chances are that it can be found on YouTube, at least in partial, if not in complete form. YouTube is known for being the resource for millions of video clips. You don't even have to resort to using a PC or a Mac to download YouTube videos, because numerous YouTube video downloader apps are available for the Fire. A search of the Amazon app store for the phrase 'youtube downloader' will reveal a number of entries. One that has been tested by this author is the Droid Youtube Downloader by KastorSoft. The app is simple to use, it does what is expected of it, and it is free. (The app is ad supported, but the ads are small and fairly unobtrusive.)

Install the app, and its operation is simplicity itself. You launch the app, and a search box appears at the top of the screen. Type a search term, tap the magnifying glass, and the app will search the entire YouTube database for videos that match your search term. Find a desired video and tap the video, and another menu appears. From this menu, you can choose to preview the video, download the file as video, download the file as an MP3 audio file, or download the file as an AAC video file. Select Download as Video, and you will see a message indicating the percentage of progress saved, then a message indicating when the download is complete.

Once the YouTube video has completed downloading, go to your Apps screen and bring up your Personal Videos app. You will see an icon displaying the starting screen of the YouTube video, and you can tap the icon to play the video.

Storing pictures & personal videos in the Amazon cloud

Under the heading of 'Where's My Data?, chapter 1 introduced the concept of cloud based storage, which greatly increases your possible maximum storage space by saving data to web servers that reside on the Internet. As far as multimedia goes, you can store your photos and personal videos in the cloud, on Amazon's cloud drive, to be specific. If you tap the Photos option on the Navigation bar and you never set up a cloud drive account at Amazon, you'll see a welcome screen like the following:

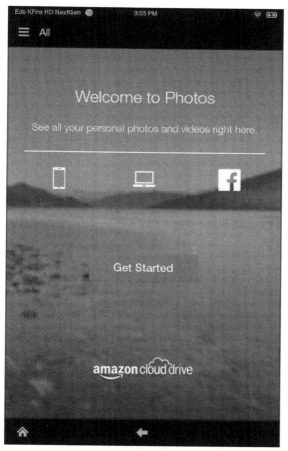

Click the Get Started link, and you will first be asked if you wish to send an app to your smartphone. (The app lets you view photos or videos stored in the Amazon cloud on your smartphone, or upload photos or videos from your phone to the Amazon cloud.) Confirm if you wish by clicking Yes and by entering your cell phone number where prompted.

Next, you will be asked if you want a link for the cloud drive app sent to your PC. Click Yes if desired, and you will receive a link via e-mail that lets you download the Amazon cloud drive app for your Windows or Apple IOS-based PC.

Once you've installed the app on a compatible smartphone or personal computer, you can move photos from your phone or your PC to Amazon's cloud drive storage.

Viewing your cloud drive photos on a Fire

After you've set up your cloud drive account and uploaded any photos, just tap Photos in the Navigation bar on your Fire. Your photos will appear in a tiled based layout like that shown in the following illustration:

You can tap on any photo and it expands to fill your Fire's screen, like the example shown:

Tap Share to share your photo via an
e-mail attachment, or via social media

Tap Delete
to delete a
photo from
the device

Tap Edit to
display the
photo
editing
tools

Tap Back to move back to the
tiled view of all photos.

You can also perform a long press (press and hold) on
any photo in your collection, and a popup menu will appear.
Your menu choices are Share, Edit, Info, Download, and
Delete.

Share lets you share the photo, either by means of an
e-mail account, or through Facebook or Twitter, if these are
linked to your Fire by means of the social settings.

Edit launches the native Photo Editor that you can use
to make changes to your photos. You can change the
brightness or contrast, crop your photo, reduce red eye, apply
filters, and apply other special effects.

Print sends the photo to a wireless printer that may be
linked to your Fire.

Info displays digital information stored about the
photo, including the filename, creation date, dimensions (in
pixels), and file size.

Download downloads the photo onto your device from the Amazon cloud, so that you will not need a Wi-Fi connection to display the photo.

Delete deletes the photo from your device.

The Amazon Cloud Storage account provides you with 5 GB of storage space, which is roughly enough to store over 2200 average photos. This amount of storage space would easily consume most of what is available on a Fire purchased with the standard 8 GB of memory. Since the Amazon cloud drive account costs you nothing with a 5 GB allotment, it is well worth your taking the time to install and use the Amazon cloud drive app.

Chapter 9: Using the Fire Cameras

One of the many features found in both the Fire HD6 and HD7 that you often won't find in under-$150 Android tablets is the inclusion of two digital cameras. Both HD model tablets include a front-facing VGA digital camera, and a rear facing 2 megapixel camera that supports 720 pixel video.

The cameras can be used to take pictures with the built-in Camera app, or with a number of 3rd-party applications available from the Amazon Appstore. You can use the cameras for video chat with the Skype app, available as a free download from the Amazon AppStore. You can also use the Facebook app to take and share photos with Facebook friends.

When viewing the Fire with its volume buttons facing to the upper right, the front-facing camera is located within the small circle at the right center of the device, as shown in the first illustration that follows. The rear-facing camera is located within the small circle at the lower right corner of the device, as shown in the second illustration that follows.

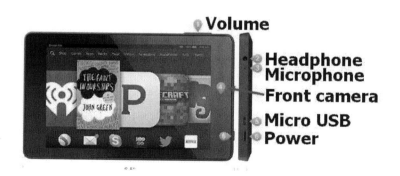

113

stereo speakers

rear camera

The front-facing camera is a VGA-resolution camera, and there is no flash included, so don't expect great results under low lighting. The rear-facing camera is a 2.0 megapixel camera that supports 720-pixel resolution (not true high definition but certainly better than standard VGA). The cameras perform adequately under average lighting conditions, and if you are using a camera app, you'll gain access to a number of user adjustable features that can enhance the quality of photos or videos. Since the front facing camera is facing towards you as you view the screen, it's clear that Amazon designed it initially to support video chatting or video conferencing with apps such as the Skype app. But since the release of the second-generation Fire line, the built-in Camera app has undergone a number of improvements, that let you do much more with the built-in cameras than just video chat, and take simple portraits, and that is the subject of this chapter.

Using the Fire's built-in Camera app

A basic camera app comes built into the Fire software, and it does a perfectly acceptable job of taking basic pictures or videos. Before taking any photos or videos with the camera, you should take the time to ensure that the camera lens is clean and free of any dust or other obstructions. Once you've done so, get to the Home screen, tap Apps, and locate and tap the Camera icon to open the Camera app. The following illustration shows the screen and the controls that are visible when you use the Camera App.

Switch between front and rear camera

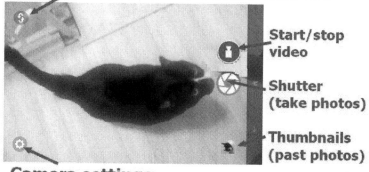

Start/stop video

Shutter (take photos)

Thumbnails (past photos)

Camera settings

(Fire camera controls. Tap the image to enlarge.)

Tap the Shutter control to take photos in Camera mode, or tap the Start/Stop Video control to begin or end video recording.

With video recording, you can pinch the screen with two fingers to zoom in, or spread two fingers apart on the screen to zoom outwards. Once recording begins, tapping the Start/Stop Video control again will stop the video recording.

TIP **With the rear camera, use the Volume buttons as a zoom control.** The rear-facing camera has a Zoom feature that is activated through the use of the volume buttons on the Fire. By default, the camera starts at 1X magnification. Pressing the volume-up button increases the magnification to a maximum of 2X (twice normal size), and once increased, pressing the volume-down button decreases the magnification.

Viewing photos with the Camera Roll

After you've taken a photo or recorded a video, you can tap the thumbnail to see your Camera Roll, which enables you to view your most recent photos or videos. You can swipe to the left or to the right to move through the photos and videos contained in your Camera Roll.

To edit, delete, or view details (such as the creation date and time of your photos or videos), tap the Menu icon, shown here.

Tap the Menu icon at the far right edge of the toolbar to open this menu.

Choose Print to send a photo to a compatible printer; Info to see the creation date and time and dimensions; or Download to download the photo to your Downloads folder.

The menu provides you with three choices: Print, Info, and Download. Choose Print to print to a compatible wireless printer (see Chapter 11 for more details about printing from your Fire). Info displays a dialog box containing information about the photo, including the date and time created, the filename, its dimensions, and the amount of memory space used by the photo. The Download option copies the photo into your Downloads directory, where it can be accessed by many other apps. (You can also use the techniques covered earlier in

Chapter 6 to copy the photo from your Downloads directory to your computer.)

Editing and Deleting Photos

When any single photo is visible on the Camera Roll, the toolbar at the top of the screen shows icons labelled 'Share', 'Edit', and 'Delete', in addition to the Menu icon. The Delete choice deletes the current photo from your device.

Tapping Edit brings up a built-in photo editor which lets you apply a variety of effects to your photo, such as changing the brightness or contrast, modifying exposure levels and eliminating 'redeye,' cropping, and adding text or drawings to a photo. While viewing any photo, tap the photo to display the toolbar at the top of the screen, and then tap the Edit icon to launch the Photo Editor. When the Photo Editor starts, you will see a menu at the bottom of the screen that displays a variety of photo editing categories, as shown in the following illustration.

Tap any category to view the editing tools for that category. If there is just one tool in a category, you will be taken to that tool. If there are multiple tools for a category, simply tap a desired tool to use it.

When you are finished editing the photo, tap Apply to save your edits. (If you decide not to use a chosen photo editing tool, swipe up from the bottom of the screen to return to the Photo Editor categories.)

When you are finished using the Photo Editor, tap Done at the upper right to exit from the app.

Sharing your photos with others

While you are displaying any photo or video in the Camera Roll, you can tap the Share icon in the toolbar area, to bring up a menu of sharing options that you can use to share photos or videos with friends. The Share icon is shown here:

Tap the icon, and a menu of choices that include Twitter, Facebook, and e-mail appears. (Additional choices may appear on this menu, depending on the apps that you have installed on your device.) You can select any of those choices to share your photos or videos by means of the Twitter or Facebook social networks, by means of an e-mail attachment, or by means of another app on your device that has photo-sharing capabilities, such as Pinterest or Instagram.

An important note about photo & video storage and the Amazon Cloud Drive

By default, all photos and videos that you take using the built-in cameras of any Kindle Fire are backed up to your Amazon Cloud Drive account. If you do not want this copying of your files to the Amazon Cloud Drive to occur, drag the menu outwards from the left edge of the screen, tap Settings, and then turn the **Automatic Updates** option to **Off**.

Getting photos from your Fire onto your computer

TIP You can copy photos from your Fire directly to your computer. One way to move photos from your Fire to your computer is to send the photos by e-mail, but there's another method that is often faster, especially when you have a large number of photos. You can transfer photos from your Fire to your computer using the following steps. First, connect the Fire to the computer using the USB cable. Open the Computer folder on your computer. (If you are running Windows, you can go to the Start menu and select Computer.)

Open the Computer folder and select Fire, then open that folder and select the Internal Storage folder. Open the Internal Storage folder and look for a folder named DCIM.

Open the DCIM folder and look for a folder named Camera. Open the Camera folder, and you will see your photos taken with the camera. Select the photos that you want to transfer to your computer, then right click and select Cut from the menu that appears if you want to move the photos from your Kindle, or select Copy from the menu that appears if you want to keep a copy of the photos on your Kindle. Finally, navigate to the folder on your computer where you want to place your photos, then right click and select Paste.

NOTE: **If you can't find your photos, try a reset.** At times, the Kindle's MediaScanner service does not see new pictures immediately. In order for photos and videos to show up, they have to be scanned and indexed by the MediaScanner service that is a part of the operating system running on the Fire. If you wait long enough, they will eventually show up, but you can force them to appear by simply restarting your Fire.

TIP ▷ **You can quickly delete unwanted photos while viewing them.** When any photo is visible, perform a long-press near the center of the photo. When a popup menu appears, tap "Delete" to delete the photo.

Adding capabilities with third-party camera apps

If you plan to make any extensive use of the Fire's built in cameras, you may want to download a camera app for your machine. While the built-in camera app provides a variety of editing capabilities, a number of third-party camera apps provide additional capabilities, such as increased zoom, special effects, delay timers, and the ability to pause and resume video recordings. A search of the Amazon AppStore for the phrase 'camera app' will reveal an assortment of dozens of apps.

(When shopping for a camera app—or for any 3rd-party app for that matter—examining the customer reviews is a wise idea, as the quality of 3rd-party apps in general ranges from outstanding to mediocre at best.)

General Camera tips

WARNING: **If you make use of an optional camera app purchased from the AppStore and your camera app has a 1080 pixel setting, do NOT try to use it with the front-facing camera!** Some third-party camera apps have a 1080 pixel setting within their video settings. This setting exists because these apps are written to run on other Android devices, many of which are based on hardware supporting the 1080 pixel resolution (such as the Fire HDX 8.9-inch model with rear-facing high-definition camera). The front-facing camera on any Fire does *not* support this resolution, and if you select such an option, the app will probably crash and you may have to restart your Fire. (While the Fire's display may qualify as high-definition, the front-facing camera does not.) If the app that you are using has an option for resolution settings, avoid any settings higher than 720 pixels.

When filming video, you may need to turn the camera "upside down." If you are using an optional third-party camera app that supports video filming, you may discover that the Fire gives proper results when the built-in camera is facing downwards, and not at the top of the device. (This behavior doesn't appear to affect all apps that support video, but it does appear to affect some third-party apps, so you may want to check the operation of your chosen app before attempting to record that all-important wedding or graduation using your Fire.)

Chapter 10: Transform your Fire with Apps

In this chapter, we look at the power of apps to add significant features and capabilities to your Fire. The tablet would be impressive if it were only used for reading books and magazines, for watching movies and TV shows, and for web browsing. But with a range of apps available from the Amazon AppStore, you can transform your Fire in an unlimited number of ways. Using apps, you can literally transform your Fire into a news or weather information center, a sports scoreboard, an international language translator, a customized radio station, a medical adviser, or a personal butler that reminds you of every appointment on your busy daily schedule. And of course, you can use an app to make your Fire into a game platform, so that you can play a few rounds of Angry Birds. This chapter will first detail various tips, tricks, and traps for apps in general, in a section we like to call 'Apps 101.' We will follow that with a listing of twenty apps that we feel that no Fire should be without.

About Apps

Apps for your Fire (or for any tablet computer, for that matter) are actually computer programs, engineered to handle a specific task. As such, they must be *installed* on your Fire, which is a sophisticated computer in its own right. You can obtain apps on your Fire by first purchasing the app (even if it's free) from the Amazon AppStore. You then install the app on your Fire by pressing the 'Download' button that appears once you purchase the app. After the app has been installed on your Fire, the download button changes to display the word 'Open', and you can press the Open button to start the app. Once the app exists on your Fire, you can get to it at any time, by choosing Apps from the Home screen, and locating and pressing on the icon for the particular app.

Before you can install an app, you will need to locate the app you want. At the Home screen, tap Apps, then at the upper right, tap Store. When the main screen of the Amazon AppStore appears, tap in the Search AppStore box at the top of the screen. The box will expand, and the keyboard will appear within the lower portion of the screen. Enter a search term to bring up one or more apps matching your search term, then tap the icon for the app that you are looking for.

Can I run generic android apps that don't come from the Amazon AppStore?

The short answer to the above question is an unqualified "maybe," but it's also a topic that is far beyond the scope of this book. You may be aware of the fact that your Fire runs a modified version of the popular Android operating system originally developed by Google. And you may be aware of the existence of android apps from other sources on the web (such as Google's own Play Store). While it is possible to run some of these apps on a Fire, it takes some tinkering with settings, and it's not a practice that Amazon recommends. Nevertheless, if you are interested in pursuing this topic further, you are definitely moving into "geek" territory. As an accomplished geek, my recommendation is that (1) you tread very carefully when journeying into this area and (2) you refer to a "geek" level treatment of the topic. I've written one such text; search the Amazon website for 'sideloading your fire edward jones' if you'd like to know more. Alternately, you can perform a Google search on the phrase, 'how to install playstore on the Fire,' and a number of articles will appear in response to the search. Some will be well-written, and others will make you regret having ever asked the question to begin with.

Deleting Apps

There will be times you'll want to delete an app, perhaps because it's not what you expected, or it is a game you've outgrown, or something better comes along. Apps are stored in two places: in your cloud storage on Amazon's servers, and on your Fire itself. When you initially purchase an app (even free apps are purchased, you just aren't charged for these), the app is stored in your personal space in the Amazon Cloud, where the app is not taking up any space on your Fire. When you press the download button that appears on the apps' icon in the cloud, it gets downloaded to the memory space of your Fire itself.

TIP **Remove unwanted apps from your Fire.** You can remove any app from the Fire by displaying all of your apps (tap "Apps" in the Navigation menu), then performing a "long press" on the apps icon, and choosing 'Remove from Device' from the popup menu that appears. The long press simply means that you press and hold your finger on the icon for a few seconds, until a check box appears over the icon. At the Home screen, press Apps to display your apps screen. When the apps screen appears, select 'Device' near the top center of the screen, to display all the apps currently stored on your Fire.

Press and hold your finger on the icon of the unwanted app until a menu appears, then select 'Remove from Device' from the menu. This action will delete the app from your Fire's memory space.

NOTE: **An app that's deleted from your Fire can still be taking up space in your cloud.** Keep in mind that deleting an app from your Fire itself does not remove the app from your storage in the Amazon Cloud. If you want to delete the app from cloud storage as well, go to your Home screen, tap Apps, and then tap 'Cloud' near the top center of the screen. This will reveal all your apps that are stored in the Amazon Cloud.

Locate the unwanted app, and press and hold your finger on the app icon until a popup menu appears, then choose 'Remove from Cloud' from the menu. *Note that deleting an app from your cloud storage at Amazon also wipes away any subscription information you may have saved in the app, so you should do this only if you are certain that you do not want to use the app in the future.*

Troubleshooting Apps

As mentioned earlier, apps are computer programs. And like all computer programs, they will at times fail to operate as promised, misbehave, or go absolutely haywire. When an app fails to operate as expected, your steps in resolving the issue will vary greatly depending on what type of behavior the app exhibited in the first place. Some app failures fall into the 'hiccup' category, in which case it may be best to chalk it up to the "evil gods of operating systems" and to move on in life. Other failures can go beyond the level of major annoyance; as an example, a camera app for my Fire recently caused my Fire's sound to stop working in all applications, and the only fix was to perform a hard reboot and completely reset my Fire to factory settings. If an app misbehaves, crashes, or completely locks up your Fire, here are some procedures that you can try, ranging in ascending order from minor (meaning, 'let's hope this works') to major (meaning, 'lets hope you don't have to resort to this')-

1. *Close and restart the app.* Without subjecting you to a heavy dose of techno-babble, let's just say that Android-based computers tend to be more stable than some small computer operating systems (Windows, not that anyone is pointing fingers) because each Android app runs in something called *protected space*. From a programming point of view, each app can "play inside its own sandbox." This means that in theory, the abnormal operation of an app should not affect the entire operating system, nor should it have an effect on other apps. When an app misbehaves, the least troublesome step is to completely close the app, then restart the app. If this does not fix the problem you can move on to-

2. *Perform a soft reset on your Fire.* This happens naturally whenever you power down the machine, so just try

turning it off. Wait 10 seconds, and power the Fire back on, then try the app again. If the soft reset fails to bring your machine back to normal operation, you can resort to-

3. ***Perform a hard reset.*** With the Kindle powered up, press and hold the power button depressed until you see a "Power off?" prompt appear on the screen. Tap 'Yes' in response to this prompt, and your Kindle will shut down. Wait 10 seconds, and power your Kindle back up. You may notice a distinct difference in the appearance of the startup sequence this time, as the 'Amazon' logo in white will appear in the center of the screen followed by the word 'fire' in orange. This simple display will remain for a short period of time (less than 2 minutes) while the machine restarts. Hopefully, this will fix the issue, because the most drastic step will also result in a definite loss of settings. But if you must resort to the most drastic step--

4. ***Reset your Fire to its default directory settings.*** Be warned that if use this last resort, you will need to reset your username and e-mail account information that you've registered with Amazon into the device, and you will have to pull all your apps back down from the Amazon cloud (and reenter any user settings that may have been stored in these apps). To perform this ultimate reboot, use the following steps:

a. At the Home screen, tap and drag down from the top of the screen, and tap Settings.

b. At the next screen, choose 'Device.'

c. At the next screen, choose 'Reset to Factory Defaults.'

If your Fire still has operational issues after this type of reset, it is definitely time to get on the phone with Amazon Customer Service.

Twenty FREE Apps That No Fire Should Be Without

As promised, here's a listing of 20 FREE apps (you heard correctly, the price is zero, nada, zilch) that this author believes should be on the carousel of every Fire. This is an admittedly subjective list, but each of these apps has also received a high average rating (between 4 and 5 stars) from Amazon reviewers. So if any of these apps suits your fancy, tap the Shop' link on your Fire, then tap 'Apps' at the left, and perform a search by name for the desired app. When the page for the app appears, you can click the 'Get App' button to download the app to your Fire.

Note that the write-ups of the 20 free apps that follow are excerpted from the publication, *Top 300 (Plus) Free Apps for the Kindle Fire* by this same author. If you would like to see the other 280-something recommendations detailed in that book, consider going to the Amazon website and spending the reasonable sum of ninety-nine cents on *Top 300 (Plus) Free Apps for the Kindle Fire* by Edward Jones.

Crackle

Crackle is an outstanding source of FREE (that's correct, as in 'no subscrber or pay-per-view fees imvolved) movies and TV shows. With the Crackle app installed on yor Kindle Fire, you get immediate access to thousands of full-length Hollywood movies and TV shows. At the time this was written, the lineup on Crackle included movies like Pineapple Express, Big Daddy, Joe Dirt, Mr. Deeds, Alien Hunter, The Deep, Panic Room, S.W.A.T., and hundreds of others. Also in the Crackle lineup are dozens of TV shows like Seinfeld, The Prisoner, Marvel Comics' Iron Man animated series, All in the Family, and Chosen, just to name a few. Twenty new movies and TV episodes are added to the lineup each month, from genres that include action, anime, comedy, crime, horror, thrillers, and sci-fi. Crackle is truly free internet entertainment at its best, and unless you only purchased your Fire for reading, you shuld definitely have the Crackle app as one of your apps.

Netflix

The app may be free, but of course you'll need a Netflix subscription to actually watch any content. Given that fact, if you are a Netflix subscriber, you'll want the free Netflix app for your Fire. You can watch all of the same Netflix videos that you might see streamed to your laptop, and if you've got a Fire, you can enjoy that Dolby surround sound which comes across nicely with a good pair of headphones plugged into the Kindle. Log in with your NetFlix account, and you can get their usual unlimited shows and flicks on your Fire, and can even pick up where you left off on a show you'd started watching earlier on your TV set or other portable device. Of course, no movie-viewing app would be complete without having the Internet Movie Database (IMDb) app so you can get a good idea of what you're watching before you decide to watch it; the Internet Movie Database app is described next.

IMDb

If you are a movie fan or a fan of regular TV shows, or even if you aren't but don't want to be embarrassed by those trivia-type TV actor questions that arise when you and your friends are debating "who played in what role," you'll want IMDb on your Fire. The app gives you access to a database of two million titles and four million cast members. It is divided into movies and TV sections, you can see what U.S. movies are getting the highest box office ratings, and you can even watch trailers for hundreds of thousands of movies. The app doesn't have anything that you couldn't get from the IMDb web site running on your laptop for desktop computer, but the interface is intuitive, the app is free, and it's easy to carry around on your Fire.

USA Today

From what multiple reviewers and this author say, the USA Today app for the Kindle Fire is the kind of app that every newspaper app should be. The content is beautiful, optimized to take advantage of the Fire's larger screen. Unlike many newspaper apps for Android-based tablets, the content is all free on this one; there are no subscription services to pay whatsoever. While you're online, the app feeds you constant updates, making sure you've received the latest news and information, and you can pull down stories for offline reading when you don't have Internet access.

The organization is logical, the formatting is colorful, and from a user friendliness standpoint it's a cinch to navigate. There is a wonderfully-intuitive 'swipe to the left or right' action within the main content viewer that automatically jumps you between stories in the smaller Articles window on the left, or you can tap any story within the Articles window to bring up the corresponding story on the right. Stories are laced with top-notch photography and occasionally with vivid video narratives. As an online newspaper, this implementation absolutely rocks. Oh, and did we mention that it's free? As a newspaper, USA Today on the Fire deserves five stars.

The Weather Channel

For the kind of in-depth weather reporting that you've come to rely on, you no longer need to turn to a cable or satellite TV channel. The Weather Channel is now no further than your Fire. Get animated and customizable radar maps; immediate, 36-hour, and ten day forecasts; severe weather alerts for the US and Europe; the ability to save multiple locations; and a "find me" feature that provides you with pinpoint local weather, based on your GPS location. Even the local pollen counts, which are often omitted from other sources, can be found at The Weather Channel. One particularly nice feature is the ability to touch a 'Video' button and get the local forecast for your area on demand from one of the TV anchors for The Weather Channel.

ESPN ScoreCenter

When it comes time to talk sports around the office water cooler on a Monday morning, you'll never be stumped for a score again if you install the ESPN ScoreCenter app on your Fire. You'll get scores, team standings, and news from hundreds of sports leagues worldwide. The variety of sports provided by ESPN ScoreCenter is just short of breathtaking- you'll find NFL and college football, NBA and college basketball, Major League Baseball, NHL Ice Hockey, and most other NCAA sports. If you are a big soccer fan, you'll find coverage of the Premier League, UEFA Champions League, the World Cup, and hundreds of additional soccer leagues and tournaments. NASCAR and Indy racing fans will find full coverage of motor sports, and golf, tennis, rugby, and cricket fans are all covered as well. If you are looking to keep up with the sports scene, you'll find it all in the ESPN ScoreCenter app.

Facebook by Facebook

This is the Facebook app for the Fire, engineered by the programmers at Facebook. It's basically the same app that was created by Facebook for generic Android-based tablets, with a few tweaks in the programming code to allow it to run under the heavily modified version of the Android operating system used by the Fire.

If you are familiar with Facebook, you have an idea of what to expect, and you do get these basics from the Facebook app. The news feed is here, and a new button at the upper right of the news feed quickly shows you who among your Facebook friends is available to message. When sending messages from within the app, you can see who is active, so you will have an idea as to when you can expect a reply. As with Facebook from the web, you can see what your friends are up to; share updates, photos, and videos; get notifications when others 'like' or comment on your posts; and text, chat, and carry on group conversations.

All that being said, the Facebook app gets a 'middle of the road' rating from Amazon reviewers, having had its fair share of teething problems. The most commonly experienced problem, according to numerous Amazon reviewers, is an inability to see more than roughly ten posts in your message wall or in the news feed. This problem has been reported to Facebook for about as long as the Facebook app has been in existence (which has been for some months now). If you install a Facebook app and you encounter the same type of behavior, you may want to uninstall the app and consider other ways to get to Facebook, one of which is mentioned in the paragraphs that follow.

<u>Calculator Plus FREE</u> by Digital Cherry, LLC

This app earned a listing in a "best free apps" article written by USA Today, and for good reason. Calculator Plus consistently earns five stars from reviewers, thanks to its intuitive interface, its feature set, and its ease of use. It is a simple calculator with just the basics, but those basics likely make for 98% of what most people need in a calculator. The app takes advantage of the Fire's large screen to present a very basic, but totally functional desktop style calculator. You get the basic keys (+), (-), (*), (/), and (%), along with a backspace key that works intuitively in concert with the calculator's multiline display, allowing you to use the backspace key to "undo" past operations. This free app is ad supported, but the ads are unobtrusive and nearly impossible to accidentally hit while using the calculator function keys.

PageOnce Money and Bills by PageOnce Corp.

CNN/Money Magazine referred to this app as "the Cadillac of money management apps," and for good reason. You can use it to organize and track your basic spending, cash on hand, bills, credit cards, and the amount of money you have placed in investments. You can keep a high-level view of what you are spending, and even pay all your bills from one location (although note that to use the bill paying feature, the app has to connect with the PageOnce servers and there is a $.30 per transaction processing fee). PageOnce Money and Bills was designed to be a one-stop money-management destination. The app also helps you break down how much of your money goes toward different types of bills each month, from credit card bills to insurance bills to utilities. You will need to enter login information for your financial accounts, but the app has been certified by TRUSTe and VeriSign, so it meets high standards for mobile security.

Checkbook

by Digital Life Solutions

When you don't need all the features of a full fledged financial analysis or personal finance program, when all you want to do is balance your checkbook, there's Checkbook. This free app won't help you with money market rates nor will it make loan analysis evaluations for you, but it will do a first class job of helping you balance as many ledger accounts, checking or savings, as you wish. You can set up multiple accounts, and you can transfer amounts between accounts, and Checkbook will keep track of your running balances. You can also choose to base your account on any one of seven different currencies. You can group transactions into over 30 different transaction categories such as mortgage, rent, groceries, car payments, insurance, and so on, and you can create your own custom categories. You can also set up scheduled transactions, so that these are automatically deducted from your account. You'll find it much easier to avoid those nasty bank overdraft charges with Checkbook running on your Fire.

HotelTonight

by HotelTonight

How often have you found yourself on a trip and suddenly due to a change of plans, you need a great deal on a hotel room? Or perhaps you're partying with friends, or a drive home is taking longer than you thought and you're tired, or you're stuck late at work and just don't want to make the drive home. Whatever the reason, HotelTonight is a great app that offers last minute pricing on a variety of hotel rooms. The deals are based on the known fact that hotels often have unused rooms that they are willing to fill at the last minute for rock bottom prices. It's worth noting that's the app gets its updates on deals from its database daily at noon in whatever time zone you're searching in. So if you're looking for a great deal on a last minute hotel room, you won't see that days' deals until after 12 noon.

Kayak

by Kayak Software Corporation

Kayak is a great multi purpose travel app for your Fire that lets you search for and discover flights, hotels, and car rentals, compare prices, and even get notification of cancellations and delays and gate information for your flights. You can also access maps of restaurants and ATMs in different locations where you are travelling. If you're in need of a last minute hotel room, or worried about a gate change or a flight delayed due to weather conditions, or need a car rental or you would just like to see a map of the airport where you're making a connection, you can now do all of this in one single app, Kayak. One caveat is that the app appears to only use Hertz as a car rental source, but otherwise, this is a great app for all things travel related.

CruiseFinder

by iCruise.com

If you are a fan of cruising, this is one app that you'll want to have on your Fire. Cruise Finder is a comprehensive cruise vacation planning app that gives you extensive information concerning over 200 ships sailing with 20 different cruise lines. You'll find thousands of itineraries complete with day by day descriptions and route maps, online pricing, availability, and booking, photos of ports, stateroom descriptions and deck plans, and even parking and map information for cruise line ports. A 'Hot Cruise Deals' section keeps you up to date with last minute pricing, and a 'My Favorites' section lets you save your favorite ships, itineraries, and cruise lines.

YP Local Search and Gas Prices (Kindle tablet edition)

by YP

When your travel is more of the local variety, out and around your own hometown, the people behind the yellow pages have brought you a great little free app called YP Local Search and Gas Prices. You can search through over 16,000,000 businesses divided into major categories like restaurants, bars, hotels, doctors, dentists, mechanics, and more. You can check out the menus from over 300,000 restaurants, and you can find the gas stations that have the best gas prices in town. You can personalize your version of the app so that it is gives you fast access to nearby businesses, restaurants, and events in your town, and you can provide your own feedback by rating local businesses (you'll need to be online to enter ratings). If you live in an area of the country where gas prices can vary wildly from one neighborhood to another, this app can be worth having just for the possible savings in gas prices alone.

Adobe Reader by Adobe Systems

If you spend a fair amount of time working with documents that are in the portable document format (pdf) pioneered by Adobe, you may as well opt for the Adobe Reader as an app on your Fire. While you can open a PDF file in the default Kindle viewer, the Adobe Reader offers more features in terms of working with PDF documents. You can make the print larger or smaller at the touch of the magnification button. You can navigate in more ways, viewing documents in a single page format, or as a continuous series of pages. And you can search through a searchable pdf for a phrase, or e-mail a pdf as an attachment, things that you cannot do with the Fire's native viewer.

One feature that would have been nice to have would be a quick way to delete pdf documents from your Fire when you are done with them. That feature is sadly lacking from the Adobe Reader app for the Fire, so you will still need to manually go into your documents directory and delete unwanted files.

<u>iTranslate</u> by Sonico Mobile

iTranslate is a great free app that does language translation. If you're a student of languages or you do a lot of international travel, you'll definitely want to have this one on your Fire. The app does a magnificent job of combining voice recognition with voice output, so you can speak and see your language. The app will translate words, phrases, and entire sentences into any one of more than 50 languages. These words of one Amazon reviewer do a great job of describing the functionality of the program:

"I am fluent in several languages and was pretty impressed with this app. I tested with a realistic tourist phrase which was fairly complex "I would like to visit your best art museum. Can you give me a recommendation and how to get there."

I selected English from the left drop down list, typed in the phrase in English, and selected the second language from a drop down list on the right. I was impressed with the translation, the grammar was perfectly correct. Next to the text there was a button which pronounced the translation. The pronunciation was excellent and sounded like a native speaker. The intonations sounded "computer generated" but completely understandable. I tested Russian and Spanish." The reviewer goes on to state that "this was the first random sentence that came to mind, I did not try to find a phrase that would be translated well. I was quite impressed with the results."

iTranslate will even let you e-mail a translated message, share it via Twitter, or copy it into memory for use with another app. Supported languages (at the time of this writing) include the following: Afrikaans, Albanian, Arabic, Belarusian, Bulgarian, Catalan, Chinese Simplified, Chinese Traditional, Croatian, Czech, Danish, Dutch, English, Estonian, Finnish, French, Galician, German, Greek, Hebrew, Hindi, Hungarian, Icelandic, Indonesian, Italian, Irish, Japanese, Korean, Latvian, Lithuanian, Macedonian, Malay, Maltese, Norwegian, Persian, Polish, Portuguese, Romanian, Russian, Serbian, Slovak, Slovenian, Spanish, Swahili, Swedish, Tagalog, Thai, Turkish, Ukrainian, Vietnamese, Welsh, and Yiddish.

My Alarm Clock Free (by Apalon)

My Alarm Clock Free is a straightforward, flexible alarm clock app that runs nicely in the background on your Fire, until it is time to do its job and wake you from sleep. There are a variety of built-in tunes that you can use as alarms, and there is also an option that lets you fall asleep to white noise, as well as support for multiple alarms. The alarm will sound even when the app isn't running, and a built-in dimming feature changes the screen brightness, to prevent unnecessary battery drain.

Inkpad Notepad for Notes (by Workpail)

When all you need is a digital notepad, Inkpad Notepad for Notes will fill the bill. It's not designed to categorize your ideas, nor build mini-spreadsheets nor organize your friends phone numbers into small databases; it just lets you take notes. It resembles a paper notepad, and you can jot down whenever notes you like. The note is automatically saved with a title that matches the first line in the note. Tap a 'Share' button at the bottom of the note to share the note via e-mail, or by sending an SMS text message to a cell phone.

<u>WebMD</u> by WebMD

In these recessionary times of spiraling health care costs and many underinsured due to circumstances often beyond one's control, it's great to have an app like WebMD. WebMD is the popular online medical reference library brought to app form on the Fire. Using the symptom checker feature, you can choose the body part that is troubling you, select your symptoms, and learn about potential conditions or issues. WebMD's exhaustive drugs and treatments database gives you information on drugs, supplements, and vitamins. A First Aid Essentials guide to medical emergencies is available offline, so whether you have a wi-fi connection or not, you'll still be able to access the treatment essentials outlined in the First Aid Essentials guide.

File Manager (by Appsolutely)

This great free app for the Fire lets you manage and browse files, open, delete, rename and move files, zip/unzip files, and send files via email. There are no banner ads and the app is completely free, based on the Open Source (Apache 2.0) License. A note of caution here: this app lets you see files that are normally hidden from your view on the Fire, and it's possible to wreak havoc if you don't know what you are doing.

Wi-Fi File Explorer by Dooblou

Assuming you have a home network with PCs attached to it, you don't necessarily have to resort to the annoyance of a cable connected between your Fire and your computer every time you want to move a file between the two. Wi-Fi File Explorer is a neat little app that lets you transfer files wirelessly. Download and install this free app on your Fire, and when you run the app, once you identify the wi-fi network used by the Fire, you'll see a display giving you a web address that you can point a browser on the computer that's also on your network. The address will include a port number, something similar to the following:
http://192.168.1.15:8000

Point your computer's web browser to the address you're given (yours will differ from this example) and you'll see a display like the following:

Wi-Fi File Explorer gives you a file explorer view of all the folders on your Fire. You can drill down into any folder, and use the Download button at the top of the Wi-Fi File Explorer window to move files from your laptop to your Fire, without the hassle of wires.

As mentioned earlier, the write-ups of the ten free apps described in this chapter were excerpted from the publication, *Top 300 (Plus) Free Apps for the Kindle Fire* by this same author. If you would like to see the other 291 recommendations detailed in that book, consider going to the Amazon website and spending the reasonable sum of ninety-nine cents on *Top 300 (Plus) Free Apps for the Kindle Fire by Edward Jones.*

Chapter 11: Printing from your Fire

The Fire is one of a new generation of Amazon Fire products that support wireless printing, allowing you to print from your Fire directly to a variety of printers. Assuming that your printer supports wireless printing, you can print emails, contact details, calendar events, photos, personal documents, and web pages from the Silk browser from your Fire Tablet.

WARNING: **You cannot print personal documents that have been converted to Kindle format (.azw) through the Kindle Personal Documents Service.**

Before you can print from your Fire, you must first download a print plugin from the Amazon Appstore onto your Fire. A list of compatible printers can be found on the product detail page for each of the plugins. The websites for these plugins are listed below; point your Silk browser at the link that corresponds to your model of wireless printer.

Epson: www.amazon.com/dp/B00ENB2CSK

HP: www.amazon.com/dp/B00EDUTGB2

Canon: www.amazon.com/dp/B00E19FB28

Samsung:
www.amazon.com/dp/B00DMZ3AM0

Ricoh: www.amazon.com/dp/B00FAX29AG

After downloading the plugin, make sure your printer is turned on and connected to Wi-Fi. You can then press and hold the item you'd like to print, and then tap Print in the popup menu that appears. Choose your printer from the list of printers that appears, tap OK, and then tap Connect. If your printer isn't listed, tap to search for additional printers, or tap to add a printer manually using the IP address of the printer. If you don't know your printer's IP address, refer to your product's user guide for assistance.

Finally, choose the number of copies you want to print, or tap More options to choose the Color Mode, Paper Size, or Orientation. Tap Print to begin printing.

What if my printer is not on the above list?

Support for wireless printing is a relatively new printer feature at the time of this writing. As a result, the above process cannot be used with many existing printers. Fortunately, all is not lost in these cases—you may not have to shell out the costs of a new printer just to be able to print on your Fire. With the right combination of apps and free services, you can print directly from your Fire. You can use Google Cloud Print, a free service that is linked to a Google account, to print to Wi-Fi printers that are compatible with Google Cloud Print. Once you set up Google Cloud Print to work with a wi-fi printer, you'll need an app like EasyPrint. You can point a web browser at the following address to reach the EasyPrint download page:

```
http://www.amazon.com/AC-JL-EasyPrint/dp/B006CV3NG4
```

First, get a Google account if you don't already have one, and set up Google Cloud Print using your Google account. You can find full instructions explaining how to do this at http://www.google.com/cloudprint. Google Cloud Print is a web-based technology that lets you print to wi-fi enabled printers via the internet. You can print to printers that are "cloud-ready," or printers that can connect directly to the internet without a connection to a computer. Using Google Cloud Print, you can also connect to older (so-called "classic") printers if they are connected to a Windows, Mac, or Linux computer with Internet access, and Google's Chrome web browser is installed and running on the computer.

Once you've set up your wi-fi equipped printer to work with Google Cloud Print, go to the Home screen of your Fire, tap Apps, tap Store, and search for EasyPrint. The app is free (it's advertiser supported, but the ads are sufficiently unobtrusive). After you download and install the app, you will need to tell EasyPrint your Google account username and password, and you will need to specify a default printer that all print jobs should be sent to. You can then use the menu bar options within EasyPrint to choose what is to be printed from your Fire. (The following illustration shows the EasyPrint app running on the author's Fire.)

You can choose documents stored on your Fire, pdf files, web pages, or documents stored on Google Drive under your Google account. As the illustration shows, you can also choose your Google accounts to be used with EasyPrint (you can have more than one Google account used by the app), you can view all print jobs sent to your printer using Google Cloud

Print, and you can view the status of your cloud-based printers (if you have more than one printer registered with Google Cloud Print).

There are other apps available that will also let you print on your Fire using Google Cloud Print. Two that are free and work well are printer model specific; they are the Kodak Document Print App (works with Kodak printers), and the Hewlett Packard ePrint App (works with HP printers). If you happen to own a Kodak printer that is cloud ready, one nice feature of the Kodak app is that it also lets you assign an e-mail address (such as 'myprinter@kodakeprint.com') to your printer. Once you assign this address, you can send emails with or without attachments to the address from any device, not just from your Fire, and the e-mail plus any attachments will be printed on your Kodak printer.

WARNING: **If you've enabled two-step verification for added security on your Google account, you are likely to have issues getting EasyPrint or any of the Google Cloud Print-compatible apps to operate successfully on your Fire.** This doesn't appear to be a limitation of the Fire; as of this writing, the author has been unable to use a Google account that has two-step verification enabled to operate with cloud printing from *any* device, including Google's own Nexus tablet. Your recommended option in this case is to set up a separate Google account, do not enable two-step verification on that account, and use the account solely for cloud printing.

Chapter 12: Security Tips, Tricks, and Traps

      Amazon has managed to marry what is basically an Android-based tablet computer with the near-flawless customer service experience that makes for shopping with the company, and the result-- the Fire product line which includes the Fire-- makes for a consumer experience that, in terms of ease of use, is hard to beat. That same design advantage, in the wrong hands, could be a major security risk. For that reason, this chapter provides some tips on securing your Fire.

      Lock your Fire. An unlocked Fire is somewhat akin to an unlocked car with the keys left in the ignition. If you lose your Fire, or the device is stolen, whoever happens to "acquire" it could read your email, access your Facebook account, and possibly order a number of expensive items from Amazon by mail before you became aware of the loss. Make sure your Fire requires a login password to prevent unauthorized users from gaining access to the machine's content. At the Home screen, pull down the Navigation bar, and tap Settings at the upper-right to display the Settings list. Tap Security, then turn on "Lock Screen Password." Enter a password, then enter it a second time to confirm.

      Make a note of your password in a secure location, if you are the type that forgets passwords. If you do lock down your Fire and you forget the password, the only way to restore operation of the device is to perform a default factory reset, which will also erase all of your existing settings and take the machine back to the factory "out of the box" condition.

      Back up your machine's settings to the Amazon Cloud on a regular basis. You can easily backup your device settings simply by using the Sync feature on the Settings screen. Every so often (perhaps monthly), pull down the Navigation bar, tap Settings, and tap the Sync icon. Doing so will not only synchronize things such as your email and contacts, but also the general settings for the device will be backed up to your account in the Amazon Cloud. This way, if the device ever needs replacing, you will save a significant amount of time as you will be able to pull your settings from the Amazon Cloud down into the replacement device.

Check out the Amazon Help Video.

Amazon has taken the time to provide a short help video on the subject of backing up your Fire. You can view the video at the Amazon web site. Point a web browser at www.amazon.com/help and at the page that appears, click "Fire, Kindle and Echo" on the left, then click "Fire HD and HDX Tablets" on the right. At the next page, under "Getting Started," click "Fire Tablet Help Videos," then click "Backup and Restore."

Restrict purchasing and browsing with Parental Controls. If you have young ones around the house that also use your Fire, may want to turn on parental controls to prevent young ones from surfing the web's more inappropriate locations, and to prevent their making unauthorized purchases as well. At the Home screen, pull down the Navigation bar, and tap Settings at the upper-right then tap Parental Controls. Change the option to ON, and enter a password twice to activate parental controls.

Decide whether you wish to restrict applications to Amazon apps. By default, the Fire is set to only permit apps from the Amazon AppStore to be installed. There is an option under device settings to allow installation of apps from unknown sources. There are pros and cons to either choice, so you'll need to determine what will work best for you. On my Fire, I allow apps from other sources to be installed, but I'm an admitted geek. If you don't know what you are doing, or if you are not fully aware of the source of the apps that you download, you may want to leave this option turned off and stick with the Amazon AppStore for all your applications. (To change this option, pull down the Navigation bar and tap Settings at the upper-right, then tap Applications, and change the 'Allow Apps from External Sources' to Yes or No, depending on your preference.)

Implementing Parental Controls

If you have young ones sharing the use of your Fire, you will probably want to turn on the Parental Controls feature. Using Parental Controls, you can set overall limits on what anyone who uses your Fire can do without the Parental Controls password. You can prevents children from making unauthorized purchases, from surfing the web, and (if desired) from playing videos, music, apps, or games. These types of content can be blocked on an individual basis, hence you might allow your children to read books and listen to music while choosing to block apps and videos.

You can use these steps to enable Parental Controls:

1. Tap and drag down the status bar at the top of the screen.
2. Tap the Settings icon at the far right to display the settings screen.
3. Tap Parental Controls.
4. Change the setting from Off to On

You will be asked to enter and reenter a password. Once you enter a password, parental controls will be enabled with the default settings, as shown in the illustration here.

The first screen of the Parental Controls provides options for web browser, email contacts and calendars, password protected purchases, and access to a second screen that lets you block or unblock specific content types. Choosing the Block option for the web browser prevents the use of the browser unless the parental controls password is entered, and the block option for E-mail, Contacts, and Calendars prevents the use of all of these features unless the Parental Controls password is entered.

The Password Protect Purchases option is also set to On by default. With this option turned on, the Parental Controls password must be entered before any purchases can be made through the Amazon store. Just below this option is the Password Protect Video Playback option. If this option is turned on, videos cannot be played on the Fire without the use of the Parental Controls password.

The 'Block and unblock content types' option, when tapped, leads to another screen with you lets you block or unblock specific content types, as shown in this illustration.

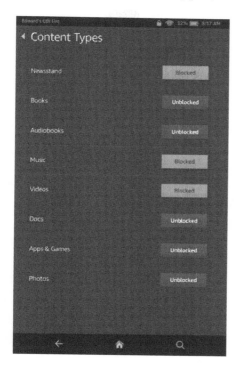

As shown in the illustration, you can choose to individually block newsstand content, books and audiobooks content, music, video, documents, apps and games, or photos, by individually pressing the button at the far right for each content type.

Finally, if you return to the first Parental Controls Settings screen and scroll upwards, you see three additional options at the bottom of the screen: Change Password, Password Protect Wi-Fi, and Password Protect LBS (Location-Based Services). The Change Password option lets you change the parental controls password (you will be asked to enter both the old and the new passwords). Turn on the Password Protect Wi-Fi option, and your children will be required to enter a password to access Wi-Fi for any reason. Turning on the

181

Password Protect Location-Based services option will then require a password to be entered before any location based services (GPS) can be accessed by any apps or other software that is installed on the Fire.

About Kindle FreeTime

Parental Controls does an excellent job of helping to safeguard younger ones in your household, but note that there is another option, Kindle FreeTime, that can go even farther in this department. With FreeTime, you can literally select the apps, videos, and reading materials that you've decided are appropriate for a child. You can also set time limits that control the amount of time your children can spend using the Fire each day. You can do this for up to 6 different children on the same Fire. This book does not delve into FreeTime in detail, but you can CLICK THIS LINK to view additional details regarding Kindle FreeTime.

CONCLUSION (and a favor to ask!)

I truly hope that you enjoy using your Fire HD6 or HD7 as much as I have enjoyed using mine and writing about both models of Amazon's Fire. As an author, I'd love to ask a favor: if you have the time, please consider writing a short review of this book. Honest reviews help me to write better books. To submit a review, go to www.amazon.com and search on the phrase 'fire hd6 and hd7 made easy edward jones.' When the page for this book appears, scroll to the bottom of the page, and click the 'Customer Reviews' link. And my sincere thanks for your time!

I do feel that Amazon's Fire is one awesome tablet, and as a technology writer I've got plenty to compare it against. In my household, there are seven Amazon tablets, (an HD6 and an HD7, a 7-inch HDX and an 8.9-inch HDX a 1st and a 2nd-generation HD, and a Paperwhite), two Barnes and Noble NOOKs, a Samsung Galaxy Tab 10, a Google Nexus, and an Apple iPad Mini. So many people think the Kindle product line is just for reading books, but machines like the Fire HD6 and HD7 can do so much more. Hopefully, after you have had the opportunity to try some of the many tips and tricks that have been outlined in this guide, you'll discover that for yourself.

-Ed Jones

Join our mailing list...

We would be honored to add your name to our mailing list, where we can keep you informed of any book updates and of additional tips or topics about the Amazon Fire tablets or Kindle tablets. Our mailing list will NEVER be sold to others (because we hate spam as much as you probably do), and the only information that we will ask you to supply is a valid e-mail address. Go to www.thekindlewizard.com and click the 'Sign up for our newsletter' link at the right.

Other books by the author: To visit the author's Amazon page for a complete list of books, point your web browser at the following address:

http://www.amazon.com/author/edwardjones_writer

Alternately, visit the author's wbsite at www.thekindlewizard.com.

Fire HD6 and HD7 Made Easy: The VISUAL Guide for the Fire HD6 and HD7

by Edward Jones

Print edition © 15 December 2014 by Jones-Mack Technology Services of Charlotte, NC.

…The end. Yes, really!